I would like to dedicate this book to all of my spiritual mentors. Thank you for pouring God's word into me. Thank you for allowing me to see that when I am weak, Christ is strong.

POWERFULLY
WEAK

In My Weakness, God Is Strong

2018

Copyright © 2018
Tribute Publishing LLC
Frisco, Texas

Tribute Publishing, LLC

Powerfully Weak
First Edition October 2018

All Worldwide Rights Reserved
ISBN: 978-0-9998358-5-2

All Rights Reserved. No part of this book may be reproduced, stored in a retrieval system, or transmitted, in any form, or by any means, electronic, mechanical, recorded, photocopied, or otherwise, without the prior written permission of the copyright owner or the Author, except by a reviewer who may quote brief passages in a review.

Printed in the United States of America.

In God We Trust.

CONTENTS

Introduction iii

Chapter 1 – Mountains 1

Chapter 2 – Who Will Go? 7

Chapter 3 – Don't Slip 11

Chapter 4 – Eyes on the Guide 17

Chapter 5 – Slip 25

Chapter 6 – Step by Step 47

Chapter 7 – Peak 57

Chapter 8 – Descend 65

Chapter 9 – Different View 83

Chapter 10 – Evidence 89

About Jillian Murphy 101

Powerfully Weak

Introduction

Weakness is something we all flee from. No one wants the word "weak" to describe them as a characteristic trait. Weakness is so frowned upon by the world we live in that we fight against it in every way.

As a little girl, I was always the overachiever in my family. I would work for days on one simple project, spending each moment with care and specific detail. I knew that when I was done, all the time I had spent would be worth it. If I didn't understand something, I could figure it out. Just by willing it, and working at something, it would become possible. This concept is not always the truth and in certain situations the opposite of how God has asked us to live our lives.

The moment that I could no longer fake it or strong arm my way to the top of academics was the day I knew I couldn't do it on my own. What did I do? I didn't go into office hours, ask for a tutor, or any other logical solution; I kept pushing. In my mind, reaching out for help was admitting weakness. Showing that I could not handle what was given to me seemed to amount to failure. I would rather struggle on my own than to reach out and ask for help.

Refusing to accept help comes from the mindset that a person should be completely independent, pulled up by their own bootstraps, and making it to the top by the grit of their own teeth. When constantly striving to prove that we are independent and that our strength comes from our own might, we forget that asking for help is okay. I think this mindset to refuse help is an awful lesson to pass down, especially as Christians.

Being weak is something that no one wants to be but is something we should strive to be as Christians. No, I didn't write that wrong, we should strive to be weak. We should place ourselves in a constant position to be vulnerable to those around us. We should align ourselves in a way where anyone looking from the outside in our lives can tell that we didn't do it on our own. The key to your story being enticing to other people who are not Christians is that it doesn't make sense!

It doesn't make sense to be willing to be in a position that is weak, but that is what we need to do. As Christians, we cast our cares upon the Lord. (1 Peter 5:7) We constantly need to surrender the weight we have accumulated over a period of time and give it all to the Lord. Being willing to break and saying, "I need to give this to You," is the constant act of a Christian.

When I was looking for colleges and had no idea where God was going to place me, I gave it to Him. Helplessly sitting in a hospital waiting room for my grandma to get out of surgery to see if they got all of the renal cancer, I gave it to Him. Patiently begging with the Lord to see my own worth after being hurt for so many years, I gave it to Him. These were all things I know that I have no control over. All things I would desperately love to control, but I can't. Think of things you would like to control. School, work, money, family, future, grades, health; all of these things and many more probably rush to your brain. Now, remind yourself what you actually have control over. My immediate reaction is to say only myself, but that isn't even true. I can't help it if I get sick with the flu or my body starts to fail me. I do not control my own future and I don't want to.

The moment that you realize that you are helplessly out of control is the most freeing moment. I learned this concept just this year, and I have never found more joy and peace in my walk with God. As I continue to write and continue to speak, people have started to ask me my advice on how to get started. Some tell me how they have ideas about books of their own to write. Others are called to ministry and want to know how I got started in ministry.

All of these people asking me for advice is humbling. At first, I started to fix my mouth to actually advise them on how to become an author, a speaker, and to get their start in ministry. Then I realized I have nothing to share. It wasn't me. I was divinely favored. I am blessed by my eternal Father, who has given me an avenue to share more about Him.

On my last day as a teenager, I was able to spend most of it talking with a group of women about the books I had written. Sitting around, talking with them, and realizing how God has impacted my life made me so emotional. One woman asked me, "How were you qualified?" She wasn't being malicious or even insulting. She wanted to see what I did that made me the person who was given this opportunity. I just stood there and I told her "I am 100% unqualified for everything I am doing, but God." She just stared at me, and then a smile grew across her face. That night, the day turned into night, and I was no longer a teenager. Laying there, I could only ponder over who I could have become, and what could have happened. What made me special?

When we head into a job that we want, we have a list of all of our qualifications, but I don't have anything to offer the King of Kings. He created me! What can I tell Him that He doesn't already know? What can I offer that He doesn't already give?

This moment is humbling to realize as Christians that we are not called to be equipped, God equips the called. We are not called to carry the weight of our sins and hurt; we give it to God. We are not called to be strong; God is powerful when we are weak. 2 Corinthians 12:9 inspired this book. Paul was crying out to the Lord three times to take the thorn in his flesh away. 2 Corinthians 12:9 is God's response to Paul, "And He said to me, 'My grace is sufficient for you. For My power is made perfect in weakness.' Therefore, I will boast all the more gladly of my weaknesses so that the power of Christ may rest upon me." God declares that His power is made perfect in weakness. There is no if, and, or but about it. God will use you at your weakest because He is all powerful.

I have a challenge for you. As you read this book, allow yourself to see the journey we all have to walk as Christians. Think of your journey that you have been on so far. The ups and the downs. The battles and the victories. Then, at the very end, think, "Am I allowing God to have full control over my life?" John 3:30 talks about the Lord saying, "He must increase, but I must decrease." Who is bigger in your life? God or you?

Let me encourage you to walk boldly as a Christian. Walk unashamed of the gospel. Live powerfully weak.

Powerfully Weak

Powerfully Weak

CHAPTER 1

Mountains

The car hummed whizzing through the mountains. I stretched my neck as far out of the window as I could to appreciate every inch of the Rocky Mountains. The cotton candy clouds above me were placed perfectly on the canvas of the pure blue sky. The true blue color made it seem like God had just painted the sky that morning. The beauty made praise escape my lips. I couldn't help but think how great God is when I looked at creation passing by. I was able to appreciate that I had an intimate relationship with the God of the universe that created me and spoke all of creation into existence.

When the car pulled to a stop, my friends and I jumped out and stood in awe. We were completely surrounded by massive mountains. One mountain, in particular, caught my eye. It was like this particular mountain puffed its chest out with its known authority. One that stood a little bit taller than all of the others.

Looking at this mountain sent me back to when I was a little girl. I remembered the days of being one of four kids in the house. We would run up next to each other and stand stiff as a board, sucking all of our height, pressing it up toward the sky, trying to see who was tallest. Every single time I would try to stretch and lengthen myself as much as possible. Unlike this mountain, I always measured up as the shortest in my family at a whopping five feet and one and a

Chapter 1 – Mountains

half inch tall. Drawing myself back into the beauty of my surroundings, I noticed that this mountain was barely taller, but it seemed to be lengthening itself to be known as the tallest within its vicinity.

As my group of friends all continued to walk around, I spotted areas of polar opposite seasons. In one area, there was full green grass dancing in the breeze, breathing out a glimpse of spring. Turning to the other side was the crisp white snow demanding winter to take its rightful place. The seasons battling each other didn't seem right. Living most of my life in Texas, I am used to mixed weather. One day the sun is beating down against your neck and the next day you are layered in as much as you can wear to hold in heat. These battling seasons that seemed to fight for dominance made me appreciate God and His creation all the more. A deep breath in… and out... I stopped and tried to soak in all of it.

Where were we? Rocky Mountain National Park. I was at a summer camp with a Bible study group. My friends and I had the great opportunity to go into the National Park and experience Colorado. Looking around, I couldn't help but allow my every step to be placed towards the mountain. The mountain towering over me seemed larger than life, taller than any skyscraper standing tall in New York City. God created this vast mountain that seemed immovable. It was so crazy to reflect on how God created the strength of this mountain and He also created me. Even though the mountain seemed to demand authority from everything surrounding it, I knew that God crafted me more delicately than it because He created me in His image.

All of the mountains seemed to be kissing the sky, and all of a sudden, we stopped in front of one. I didn't understand why we stopped in front of this particular

Chapter 1 – Mountains

mountain, but we did. It was the same one that seemed to demand its authority consistently. In the grand scheme of things this mountain was far from the biggest, but it seemed to draw my attention. I mean it had caught my focus all day.

My friends and I looked at the leader as we stood still. We all knew that he had brought us from our campgrounds to hike a mountain, and we all looked at him expectantly. He didn't miss a beat and told us that we were going to hike and climb this mountain.

My first rush of emotion was to look at the mountain and to become very excited. I knew it would be difficult to hike and climb the mountain, but the guide chose this particular mountain. How hard could it be? He knew our skill level and these mountains; we had nothing to fear. All I needed to do was enjoy the climb and enjoy being at the top once I got there.

It is funny to look back and truly analyze this moment. Riding into Rocky Mountain National Park, an area so rich of God's goodness, allowed me to praise Him. In everyday life, I don't stop to soak up the beauty He created around my home. I don't stop and look in the mirror and appreciate that I was made in the image of God. My world is so fast-paced, but in a moment when it seemed that I had no other choice but to face it, I was in awe. It made me stop.

When I was a little girl soaking in the sun, I remember sitting and asking my mom, "If someone never hears the Word of God, how will they learn about Jesus?" I was concerned because I knew that we had the responsibility to share the gospel with others, but the world seemed

Chapter 1 – Mountains

endless. How could we all get to every crevice of the earth to share God's love?

My mom explained to me, "Everyone will be able to experience the Lord. In some cases, it is through you and me. In other cases, it is God's creation praising Him that allows everyone to know there is a God who created all that they see, hear, feel, and taste."

Wondering how people would come to know Jesus Christ led me to 1 Chronicles 16:31-33, "Let the heavens be glad, and let the earth rejoice, and let them say among the nations, "The Lord reigns!" Let the sea roar, and all that fills it; let the field exult, and everything in it! Then shall the trees of the forest sing for joy before the Lord, for he comes to judge the earth." As I rode into Rocky Mountain National Park, I wanted to strain my body to see every inch of God's beautiful work and it caused praise to be released from my lips. This is the same way that creation will sing the praises of the Lord. For someone who has never met a person who knows of Christianity or of God, they will know the beauty of creation. Creation does sing the praises of the Lord. Why? God spoke all of creation into existence, and they can't help but to praise Him. If creation sings the praises of the Lord, so should we.

As humans, we were given the privilege of choosing. God loves us so much that He didn't even force us to choose Him. He wanted us to come to Him on our own. God gave us the right to choose to follow Him, or to struggle in finding our own way. He placed in us a God-shaped hole. This hole drives us to strive to fill it, but nothing can fill it but Jesus Christ. Many people drown out the void with people, possessions, and power. All of the p's will not hold eternal weight. They will all fade. The God-shaped hole will prevail.

Chapter 1 – Mountains

The beautiful difference is that as Christians, God fills the void inside of us. God gives us a new purpose and a new hope in Him. We are able to rest in God's grace and truth. The love of God is unmatched and surpasses all. He is the one who crafted us together in our mother's womb as the Bible says in Psalm 139:13. God is the one who planned out our lives before we even took our first breath and meant it for our welfare. God is the one who knows everything we have ever done, but still has His arms opened wide, right where we are at. He loves us and wants us so much. His love is unimaginable, and standing in the midst of the massive mountains, I got a taste of how God is truly the Almighty King.

When I look at God in context of all that He created, I can't help but wonder, why don't I trust Him? Being completely honest with my feelings and apprehensions, why don't I fully rely on God? I look back to myself in the midst of the Rocky Mountains and see the unearned trust I put into my guide.

During my adventure in the Rocky Mountains, not once did I ask the guide how many times he had led a group. I didn't even ask if he had led a group before. When he chose the mountain, we were going to hike that day I did not even question him. I had no apprehensions, no worries, only excitement. This guide did nothing to prove himself, yet I trusted him with my life.

God has proved himself time and time again in my life. From the smallest prayers: before a test, for safe travels, for a good day, to the impossible: to be able to be healed from tumors on my ovaries, to be able to have kids, to be able to take off the bondage of shame in my life and work in ministry; God has proven Himself in mighty ways time and

Chapter 1 – Mountains

time again in my life. Yet I question Him time and time again. I question His character as if He is not the Almighty God. I wonder if I should take pieces of my life back from Him. As if He doesn't already have full control and know the end of the story before it has even begun. I didn't give myself the full ability to let all my worries go and trust in the Savior of the world because for some reason, in the moment I thought that I knew more than He does. I was so far off that it is crazy to even comprehend. The fact that I thought I knew better than the all-knowing God of the universe is something I continually struggle with. I struggle with the ability to fully trust and fully surrender my whole life to the King of Kings.

It is not like I need God to prove Himself one more time for me to believe, I do believe. It is not like God has failed me, God never fails. I truly needed to learn how to put my blind faith in God like I did with the guide to climb the mountain. Even more than that, Christianity isn't blind faith. God made it where I know that He knows my every direction before I even spoke a word. If anything, placing my faith and trust in God is the most secure and guaranteed thing I could ever do. And placing my full faith in God was exactly what I needed to do to claim victory over the story that was already written for me.

Chapter 2

Who Will Go?

As my friends and I started walking closer to this massive mountain, the bigger it became. Every step slowly diminished the excitement in me and transformed it into worry. Closer and closer until finally, we were right next to the massive mountain, looking up, trying to see where it touched the sky.

Little five-foot-one-and-a-half-inches-on-a-good-day me stood next to one of God's most vast and beautiful creations. This put into perspective just how small I was. The rush of energy inside me evaporated into the air and I was no longer excited to hike and climb this mountain.

None of us in the group said anything. We just stopped and looked at the guide. Then, we all shifted our focus and stood staring up at the mountain, straining our necks to see the end. It seemed like the mountain just grew and grew into the air forever. We all looked back at the leader as if to say, "You expect us to climb something this massive…" The leader must have realized that we were all staring at him yet again, walked straight through us, and started to hike up the mountain. No words, only actions.

Without any kind of thought, I started hiking up the mountain behind the guide as if my natural instinct was to follow the leader. It seemed that my natural bent was to trust in the expert. One other girl joined us in the hike and the rest

Chapter 2 – Who Will Go?

of the group stood still at the bottom of the mountain. Their hesitation that led to their decision to stay at the bottom of the mountain was forfeiting their purpose of being here. Fear wedged its way in and held most of the group as captives.

    I have heard multiple times that "hindsight is the best sight." In this case, looking back on my group, it amazes me how fear can place a wedge between a group of people. Facing what seemed at times to be the Goliath of the mountains, handpicked for us, I could see why some people held back. They let their fear, worry, or doubt take control. If they would have spoken out against their fear, if they would have spoken out against their worry, or their doubt, they would have seen the mountain more objectively. They would have seen the vastness of the mountain like a little kid trying to grow a couple more inches. Their fear would have started to diminish if it was brought into the light.

    In 2 Timothy 1:7, Paul writes to Timothy saying, "For God gave us a spirit not of fear, but of power and love and self-control." In this verse, Paul is encouraging Timothy to cast out fear in his life and to replace it with power, love, and self-control. We are not meant to live our lives in a state of fear. We should hold the courage that we have in Jesus Christ close to our hearts, and when we feel fear creeping in, we know that we can place our hope and our faith in Jesus Christ.

    In each of our lives, no matter how young or how many days we have lived, we will have to face obstacles in our lives. Some obstacles we can see right before us, like the mountain facing my group to climb. Other obstacles sneak in out of nowhere and seem to hold us captive. The reassuring part of knowing you will face obstacles in your life is that once you become a Christian, you have the Holy Spirit inside of you to guide you. God did not make us and then abandon us. God is with us in every moment of each day. He is our constant help in times of trouble. God gives us His unconditional love and eternal peace in times of sorrow. God will always be there for you through it all. As a believer in Jesus Christ, we are more in tune to follow His exact steps instead of following our own path. We know that God can give us a spirit of courage and not of fear. We know that God can give us His power to face the temptation, trial, or hurt that seems to be a towering mountain before us. God will give us the "equipment" necessary to be successful on our journey; we just need to fully trust in Him.

Chapter 2 – Who Will Go?

Chapter 3

Don't Slip

In our everyday lives, we have to face a hard truth: not everyone will stand with you through the thick and thin. When you find yourself at a bump in the road or a hard time in life, it is vital to recognize which people come with you along the way and who stays behind.

People who do not sincerely care about your well-being will not want to be a part of the hard work and effort that is needed to overcome the obstacle that you are facing in life. They will want to sit back and find out "how it was" when everything is done with. We need to identify these people in our lives and be very aware. I found this out by something as simple as climbing one of the Rocky Mountains.

Looking back at this experience of hiking and climbing a mountain, I realized that I mindlessly followed after my leader. My natural bent was to follow after the one who was a certified expert in the area. I was willing to give the guide my trust in getting me to my final destination. For the other people in my group who came with us to the mountains, this was not their natural bent. Their natural bent was to sit back and wait for us to climb the mountain and come back to report how it was. They needed to see it for themselves and did not want to trust that everything would be okay. Ultimately, some people chose not to place their

Chapter 3 – Don't Slip

trust fully in the guide. The lack of trust and not being willing to relinquish control were two areas of weakness that they would need to work through.

Three of us continued to walk up the mountain without the others and it was a moment of loss, a moment of parting. Then the leader shouted, "Follow my exact step!" My mind started to focus back on the task at hand, hiking and climbing the mountain. Then, I started to wonder, "Why do I have to follow his exact step?" Sure enough, the answer to my internal question was given as I watched our leader. Along the way he was checking for loose rocks. Some of the rocks were sturdy and others would fall off the mountain immediately when there was a little pressure applied to them. I realized, he was keeping us safe. He wanted us to follow his path carefully because he didn't want us to get hurt.

I bet y'all can already see where I am going with this, but in life we have a guide. Our guide is better than any certified climbing expert. If you are a Christian, your guide through life is Jesus Christ. He knows the plans he has for you and they are for your good. Jesus is checking each step we take so that we don't have to fall.

While climbing the mountain, my natural bent was to follow. Now, don't get me wrong, my personality is of a leader, but I can recognize my strengths and weaknesses. I had never climbed a mountain on my own before, that would not be an area of strength, so I needed to fall into step with someone who could help me climb that mountain.

Chapter 3 – Don't Slip

In a way, it is funny to me to think that we have God's living word that can direct and guide each of our steps, but we still struggle with decisions. We still struggle with what to do and what not to do. Even if you are a skeptic of the Bible, you can see that the principles that Jesus teaches are inherently good. But as Christians, we know that it is so much more than that. The Bible is God's Word and is God breathed. (2 Timothy 3:16-17)

When we spend time in God's word, we are actively growing in our relationship with God. Those who decided not to follow into step with the guide immediately may be those who don't feel like joining in at this time. The thing is, timing is everything. The way we feel needs to be set aside. Emotions are tricky things and are not to be relied on. If you don't feel like reading your Bible when you wake up in the morning, that is nothing but pure laziness or false busyness stemming from Satan. That is a slippery stone placed in your life and God is telling you to not fall for it.

The reason not spending time with God is such a slippery slope is because there is no middle ground. Either you are growing steadfastly towards the Lord or you are not. When you choose to slip on that seemingly little rock, you come to find out that your fall will be farther than you thought it would and hurt more than you thought it could. In Revelations 3:15-16, the Bible says "I know your works: you are neither cold nor hot. Would that you were either cold or hot! So, because you are lukewarm, and neither hot nor cold, I will spit you out of my mouth." The Lord is disgusted with lukewarm. As Christians, we should be on fire for God and the more we live, the more we can see God's hand in every area of our lives. This is why I don't even see reading my Bible as an option. I don't see going to church as an option. I don't see prayer as an option. I see these things as flourishing my relationship with God. When you see God as an option, you are making your choice clear. You are either running towards God, or you are running away from Him.

Sitting back and trying to discover if the Christian thing is the choice you want to take or if it works or not may be a chance you are willing to take, but I am not. I see the sense of urgency in the message of the Lord. I see the excitement of what the Lord has done so far in my life and I don't want to be idle about my passion for the Lord in my fleeting time in my temporary home.

Maybe you are thinking, "Why does she have such a passion for a God that she can't see? Why should I change my life and my daily routine? Why should I allow the God of the universe to enter into every crevice of my life? Why should I give Him the burden that I have been carrying and that I am in control of?" The incomprehensible work of the Lord is why. He can take your life and turn it into something greater than you could ever ask or think. Let me tell you what He has done in my life.

One slippery rock that God allowed me to face in my life was being sexually molested for three years as a little girl. I remember when I wasn't even able to say out loud or write out what had happened. I was so covered by the guilt and shame that it seemed that I would be trapped in a fog for the rest of eternity, waiting, waiting to see the end of my hurt. Waiting still to see if my worth would ever be given back, if what was stolen would ever be replaced.

The good news is by the grace of God my story doesn't end there. Slowly by the redeeming power of God, I

Chapter 3 – Don't Slip

am healing. All the pressure being placed on my life wasn't meant to crush me. Oh no, it was meant to mold me into a beautiful creation and vessel to be used for the kingdom of God. The Bible says in Isaiah 64:8 "But now, O Lord, you are our Father; we are the clay, and you are our potter; we are all the work of your hand." I don't know how much you know about pottery, but when I first read this, I didn't know much. I learned that the potter has clay that he or she shapes to form a vessel. The thing is, the clay has to be centered, and when the clay is centered, that is when the potter starts to apply pressure. The potter applies pressure, water, and heat to start to shape the clay into a beautiful work of art. In the end, the potter has created a magnificent vessel. The thing is, just like the verse says, God is the potter and we are the clay. Don't think for a moment that when the potter is shaping the clay that it doesn't hurt. But the pressure, water, and heat being applied are necessary for the beautiful work of art the clay becomes. The same thing goes for our lives. The pressure and the hurt that we go through as Christians is difficult to make sense of, but in reality, it is God molding us in an amazing vessel.

I used to not be able to say one word about what happened because I was still wearing the bondage and weight of what had happened to me. I falsely believed that what happened was my whole story, but in reality, it was just a chapter. God had and still has so much planned for my life. What I thought was all-consuming hurt in my life was really pressure being applied for God to mold me into a vessel to be used to share the gospel. The thing is, there is something unspeakable in everyone's life. It may be the same kind of hurt, or it may be something completely different. It may be something that was done to you, or it may be something that you have done. Whatever your unspoken hurt is, I am telling

Chapter 3 – Don't Slip

you that it is your slippery rock. It has the potential to keep you down if you let it, but you have another choice. Your pain is bondage that could keep you captive; if you choose to stay captive. You have another choice, and His name is Jesus.

Our God is one who can transform a little girl who didn't even want to dream about who she could become anymore into a person who is on fire for God. This transformation is nothing short of a miracle, and I get a front row seat in watching all that God can do. So while you still have all of your doubts and questions held to your chest, realize that you are hesitant about your Creator. You are hesitant of the God who can cast out fear. You are unsure of Jesus Christ who is the Savior of the world and the eternal hero in my story. He could be in yours, too, if you let Him.

CHAPTER 4

Eyes on the Guide

What seemed to be hours later, we were probably a quarter of the way up the mountain and it was becoming increasingly more difficult to stand upright while hiking. There was no path or trail; we could only follow the leader as if we were back in elementary school following the line out to recess. Then, we stopped. The guide was gifting us with a break to drink some water. As I started to catch my breath, I looked behind me to see how far we had come, and everything seemed to be a little smaller. Looking up, I could not even see the top of the mountain anymore.

After resting for a little while, the guide asked if we were ready to continue. We said yes. I started to try and stand up to start walking again, but he told me to wait. I waited and watched him. He told us that we are getting to the point where we won't be able to stand upright. We shouldn't even try to. We need to crawl. When he said crawl, I immediately started to picture images of little babies crawling around on the floor. This image was interrupted by the leader explaining; it will be like a bear crawl since we are focused on moving up the mountain. The only time I had ever had to do a bear crawl was up and down the court for talking too much in PE in middle school. I guess I would reteach my body to do it today.

We began to crawl, again slowly following right behind the leader. At some point, the girl with us asked us to

Chapter 4 – Eyes on the Guide

stop. We stopped, and she began to cry. She said that she thought this would be fun and a cool adventure, but this is far from what she had planned. Internally, I was like "Preach. I did not expect to be sweating as much as I am, or breathing as heavy as I am." Our leader looked her straight in the eyes and told her, "We can let you sit here and quit if you want to. If you want to stay, that is okay. But know that you will miss out on the beauty of the peak." I was puzzled because I understood that we were climbing one of the Rocky Mountains and that it was really cool, but we had already hiked other way smaller mountains back at camp. I didn't understand why he emphasized this mountain. It was almost like he knew that this mountain had something extra special in store for us. Despite his warning that she would miss out, she chose to wait where she was.

I just want to thank God for giving us the choice to follow Him. We are created in God's image. Knit together in our mother's womb. The Lord knows what is best for us, but He loves us so much that He allows us to choose our own path.

Heading up the mountain, the girl with me chose not to continue, even though it was against what the guide had instructed. She was given the power to say yes or no. She was given the decision. The decision was not made for her. She had the power over herself to live according to what was advised or not.

I think that is what is amazing about the Lord. He loved us so much that He gave us free will. Free will to come back to Him and pursue a relationship with Him or to

Chapter 4 – Eyes on the Guide

choose not to. At the end of the day, we will all cry out that Jesus is Lord, but we are given the choice right now. (Philippians 2:11)

When I think of my Heavenly Father giving me the choice to pursue Him or not, I start to think of the choices I have made in my life. Some big choices I have made were where to go to college and what major to pursue. Focusing on this reminds me of the day I was dropped off at college. My mom and I drove from Texas to Oklahoma to drop me off. We were welcomed with so much spirit that I was on cloud nine heading into my room. When we saw my room and saw all my stuff, we immediately went into work mode to get my room in order.

Throughout the day, there were Bible studies and welcome meetings. I was getting to meet new people that would later become some of my best friends. Then the time came to say goodbye to parents. Well, my mom was still finishing the last details of my room. We both have the mentality to keep going until a task is done. I went into my dorm that would be my new home for the school year, walked down the hall, and into my room. When I walked into my room, my mom immediately started to tell me how we were completely done. My eyes caught hers and immediately I started to cry.

I knew I was heading into a great time of my life. College is a great time of change and development. I knew with everything in me that I made the right choice of colleges. I walked over to my mom and she held me. She held me tight to her and she started to cry, too. I will never forget the final advice that she gave me. "Jillian, please talk to someone… and iron your clothes."

Chapter 4 – Eyes on the Guide

My mom, who knew me better than anyone else, knew I had trouble talking with people initially. My personality is slow to warm. Either I am immediately comfortable and loud, or I have to slowly warm up to people. Her second advice may seem silly, but I definitely never iron my clothes. During my college experience, I have ironed my clothes once.

My mom and I look back at my move-in day for college and we laugh. We laugh at the fact that her advice was so simple. Make friends and iron your clothes. These simple tasks may seem really easy to one person, but they are challenges for me.

As I continued up that mountain, I knew that I would be able to keep going. I recognized that my body was getting tired and possibly even a little weak, but I knew I would make it. The way I viewed the challenge of climbing up this massive mountain was not the same way my friend viewed it.

I bring this up to show how we are all at different stages of life. Some of us handle difficult circumstances like grief or pain in different ways. I don't believe that she was wrong not to continue. It was her personal choice. That is the beauty of being individuals; we have the choice to choose what we will or will not do.

With that choice, we have to take ownership. I have to own that I don't iron my clothes. I have to face the potential consequences of my actions or try to find a possible solution. In this case, my solution was to buy a steamer. The gravity can be heavier in other situations that are different than climbing a mountain or ironing.

Chapter 4 – Eyes on the Guide

One of the stories I love about choice is Esther. You should definitely read the book of Esther, but right now I will give you the spark notes version. Esther was an orphan raised by her cousin Mordecai. She is a Jew and ends up becoming the Queen of Susa in Queen Vashti's place. After she becomes the Queen, Haman, who was the right-hand man to the King, decides to make a decree to eliminate the Jews. Haman does this because Mordecai refuses to bow to Haman in the courts of the kingdom. Esther finds out that her cousin Mordecai was mourning and sends a servant to talk with him. Mordecai then sends a message to Esther to go to the King and to save the Jews. Esther at first sends a message back to Mordecai that she can't because she has not been called to see the King, and if anyone enters into the King's courts without being summoned they will be killed unless the King decides to spare their life. Now we are all caught up through Esther 4.

Esther 4:12-14 says "And they told Mordecai what Esther had said. Then Mordecai told them to reply to Esther, 'Do not think to yourself that in the king's palace you will escape any more than all the other Jews. For if you keep silent at this time, relief and deliverance will rise for the Jews from another place, but you and your father's house will perish. And who knows whether you have not come to the kingdom for such a time as this?'" Mordecai is allowing Esther to see her choices. He wants her to see that she will not escape the persecution facing the Jews and if she decides to say no, that God will use someone else. God is not limited to only using her. This is true for Esther and true for our lives as well. Then, Mordecai allows her to see a second option. The option that God had placed her as Queen to save the Jews.

Chapter 4 – Eyes on the Guide

If you know the story of Esther, you know that she chooses to go to the King. She was given a choice. Yes, God positioned her as the Queen of Susa. Yes, to us it is obvious that she is supposed to go before the King. Yes, she should want to follow God's will for her. The sad thing is that while reading the story it is so black and white what she should do, but in our own lives, there is so much grey.

We don't know what choices to make. We don't know if we are in the right job. We don't know if we chose the right college. We don't know if our vocation is correct. We don't know. We see so much grey in our lives because we are looking at it all too closely. We need to back up and look at the situation from an eternal perspective.

You may be asking yourself, "What is an eternal perspective?" An eternal perspective is taking steps back from the situation you are in and deciding if it has eternal weight or not. Let's try this out. I may study for an exam in school, take the exam, and fail. What should be my reaction? I know my initial reaction would be to think that the sky was falling. It would feel like a huge deal at that time. Now, that is not looking at it from an eternal perspective. If I looked at the situation with a different lens, I could quickly see that I would need to calm down and realize it was just an exam. Yes, I said it. Just an exam. That exam has no eternal weight. I should go talk with the teacher to see how I can improve. I should study harder and possibly join a study group. I should view it as a lesson that revealed what I need to improve. I should make some changes due to my result, but it is still just an exam.

My whole point is that we have the power to choose how we respond to situations. We even have the power to

Chapter 4 – Eyes on the Guide

view our situations in black and white if we hold them up to the lens of whether it has eternal weight or not. Think, "Does it matter in the grand scheme of things to further the kingdom of God?" If not, take a deep breath and work your way through it.

As Christians, we need to be able to make solid decisions for our lives and own up to our decisions. We have a choice on whether to have a relationship with our Lord and Savior Jesus Christ or not. I hope we all have made the decision to follow Him. Then, we are faced with another choice. A choice to follow God's will for our lives or not. A choice to actively pursue God daily or not. A choice on whether to treat each person we come across with love or not.

I can tell you right now that Esther did not take her decision lightly whether to go before the King. She saw the eternal weight. She saw her possible death versus the impending death of all the Jews. That probably made her decision very clear. We have the choice to share God's Word or not to. So many people around us are spiritually dead. We have the choice to share God's unconditional love with them or not. We get to decide whether we will be faithful in sharing the gospel with others or not. Even though the weight of this choice is heavy, it is simple to me. That is probably because I can't keep quiet about all that God has done in my life.

Now that we know that our worlds are filled with choices, I pray that you choose the right one. Even though we all get to make our own choices, there is such a thing as a right and a wrong choice. I hope that we choose to make the right choices along the path that God has laid out for our

Chapter 4 – Eyes on the Guide

lives. Whether the choice is simple or heavy, I pray you choose the right one.

Chapter 5

Slip

The higher we climbed, the more it felt like I was on a rock climbing wall than a hike. I continued to grab on to the mountain and just follow the guide's exact placement. I wasn't even enjoying the climb; I was mentally and physically exhausted. Right foot here, left hand there. Follow the guide's exact placement. Left foot here, right hand there. The more I climbed, the more I thought about how it was like an intense game of Twister. As long as my body completely followed the guide, I would be okay. I knew there was nothing to fear.

In that exact moment, I placed my foot on a different rock than the guide's, and before I could even realize what was happening, I was slipping down the mountain. My foundation literally fell from underneath me. All of a sudden, I stopped falling. My heart went back up to my chest. I started to breathe heavily and quickly looked up to where I was going and back to where I could have kept falling. I was trying to mentally understand what had just happened.

I kept thinking, "I thought I was following the guide. I thought I was right where I needed to be, but I took one wrong step and it resulted in a few scrapes and bruises." In that moment, I didn't want to continue. I looked back down and towards the top again. It seemed like I was closer to the top than the bottom, but I didn't care. This was the sign that I was in over my head and that I needed to quit now.

Chapter 5 – Slip

Then, I heard the guide ask me, "Jillian, are you alright? Are you ready to continue?" Ready to continue? I almost died! My entire body just slid down the mountain, and you think I am just going to keep on climbing? This is ridiculous. I looked at him, and said, "No, I'm not ready. I am going to head back." The guide didn't say a word, but it was like a whisper came from the wind, advising me, "You are too far up to turn back now."

I took a deep breath and let myself wallow. I kept giving myself a head-to-toe check to the best of my abilities. Then I reluctantly looked up at the guide and said "Yes, I'm sorry. I am ready now."

The climb up after the slide was cautious and every move hurt. Nothing was broken, I was just scraped and bruised. With each move towards the top, trying to follow his exact path just made me grow weary. I was so tired and everything in me wanted to give up in that exact moment. Still, I kept moving, eyes locked on my guide, determined to follow and not to fall. After the bumps in the road that I had to overcome, I was determined to reach the peak.

Keep climbing. Stay in tune with his exact path. Keep going up. Push. Don't stop. Keep your eyes locked on the one who knows the way.

One summer day, I remember leaving a mission trip meeting understanding the importance of reaching people who don't know Christ and the importance of explaining that they can have a personal relationship with God. Whether the people we minister to believe that at first or not,

Chapter 5 – Slip

it is a blessing to plant a seed in their hearts, a seed that could one day flourish into a relationship with Jesus.

The meeting entailed a lot of information on how to tell the gospel. These were things that I knew deep inside my heart, but I still listened. Tell them the name of the one who created them in His own image. The name of the one who loves them despite everything they have done. The one thing in the meeting that I couldn't wrap my head around is how you could visually see spiritual battles. The mission trip sponsor was warning us that where we were going, you could visibly see spiritual battles happening.

Don't get me wrong, I have seen how satan can tear up a family on the way to church on a Sunday morning. The kids don't want to wake up, you feel sick from the activities from the night before, arguments, bad hair… it goes on and on. At the heart of this conflict is satan trying to place obstacles in your way to not allow you to hear God's word in the midst of a community of believers who will hold you accountable to living out your faith in your day-to-day life.

But I still couldn't fully grasp the concept of seeing a battle before me. I could grasp the church scenario, of course, but a full-blown battle? How? Where? What? All these questions were popping into my mind and I was praying that I wouldn't have to fight. I didn't want to be the one who had to fight in a spiritual battle. I was heading towards the end of summer break and going into my sophomore year of college. I didn't need to be in the front lines against anything. I kept praying to God not to allow anything to happen where I would have to fight. Then, a calm washed over me. Just like when you go to the beach on a beautiful sunny day, you sit at the edge to test out the water.

Chapter 5 – Slip

You sit and let the first wave roll up and engulf your legs and fall back. It was like God engulfed me in His loving peace without me having to say anything else. I sat there like this for a while. Then, I got up and left the meeting without having a worry in the world about the trip.

My mom came to me later that night. She was talking to me about how I really needed to stay with the group and not go off and share the good news alone. She advised me to keep my guard up. I remember how worried she was. She was beating herself up about not having a passport ready just in case she needed to come and be there for me. She was getting the feeling that I was about to walk into a spiritual battle. I remember looking at her and telling her with a smile on my face, "Mommy, I will be more than okay. I promise." She was still very worried, but I am her baby girl. Her baby girl that she was sending across the world to share about how amazing our God is, how He has changed my life, and how I would not be standing there or even living without Him. I knew she was proud, but I also knew she had a huge fear of being powerless when it came to her baby girl. I knew God would take care of me. She knew that, too.

The next morning, I held her hand the whole way to the airport. It was like I was a little girl holding tight to my mommy before the first time walking into school, wanting to remember her touch and love while I was gone. I knew she would be one of my hardest goodbyes. More than that, I knew she would be my prayer warrior. I knew if my mommy was praying over me and I was praying over this trip, then I would be safe. I was heading into a spiritual war zone and I felt covered. I knew, without a doubt, I was safe and protected in the arms of my Eternal Father. I am going to do His work that He called me to do. I would be His hands and

Chapter 5 – Slip

feet, and seeing how He chooses to move in a different country would be more than rewarding.

My mom walked with me and the rest of my group until we had to go through security. Then, she had to go. I walked through security with my new team that I would serve with. My new family, brothers and sisters in Christ, willing to go across the world to share the good news of Jesus Christ.

I tried to stay focused. Focused on the eternal purpose of this trip; the impact that was about to be made. All the while, I had fun meeting the girls I was going with. I could almost feel all of our energy and anticipation building. Finally, it was time to board the plane. We were boarding the first plane of our trip, and it would be the longest flight. We were about to sit in a flight for sixteen hours, and all I could think about is how I could possibly pass the time.

I filed onto the plane with the others and we were all spread throughout the plane. I sat in the middle seat. In the window seat was a man. He seemed nice; we didn't really talk. On my other side was a girl from our mission trip team and she was sitting in the aisle seat. We talked for a long time about college, the trip, etc. Then, we both started to watch movies.

I remember looking out the window and slowly seeing the sky transform from a mixture of reds, oranges, and yellows to a blue-black. This sky would eventually go pitch black.

How long will this flight last? It seems like I have been on this plane forever. I started watching movies on my

Chapter 5 – Slip

screen, but I was so bored. I was just trying to pass the time. I would constantly check how many more hours the flight had left.

They brought us food, but I wasn't very hungry. I guess I was still so excited about the trip. It all felt like a dream, not like I was really flying to Southeast Asia, but I was. After zoning into a movie for so long, I remember thinking, "I need to stand up and walk the aisles. Everyone told me you couldn't sit too long." I asked the girl next to me to let me out and I just started walking the aisles. I kept wondering about the people I was going to meet. I kept praying that God would give me the words to say, that nothing would be lost in translation. Then, I started to pray over the people in the plane, and I wondered if we would get to share about Jesus with any of them.

I sat back down, and slowly the plane went pitch black. You could see a few screens lit up, but most everyone was getting ready for bed. The airline was so kind to give us all blankets. I snuggled up in mine and tried to go to sleep.

I never thought of praying to have a good night sleep on the plane because I knew my number one talent was being able to sleep anywhere and at any time. When my family and I first moved to Texas, my mom hustled us all into a closet that went underneath the stairs. We were experiencing our very first tornado. My mom was consoling my siblings and she couldn't find me. She looked deeper in the corner of the closet, and in the midst of our very first storm, I was asleep tucked in the corner, totally peaceful, knowing that I would be okay and had nothing to fear.

Chapter 5 – Slip

As I started to drift off to sleep, tucked in my seat, I knew I was completely safe, and when I woke up, I would be closer to my final destination.

All of a sudden, I felt something like a spider crawling on my leg. I was terrified. I instantly woke up and jerked from my seat. I didn't get far since I still had my airline seatbelt on. I unfastened it, took off my blanket, and shook it out. I was seriously disturbed. I hate the feeling of crawling.

Tucking myself back in my blanket, I started to drift off to sleep. Then, I felt it again... the crawling. I knew there was no way a bug survived my shaking out of that blanket. I refused to open my eyes and told myself it was just the memory of the bug crawling on my leg, nothing more and nothing less.

The crawling continued, but I still refused to open my eyes, knowing at any second I could fall into a deep sleep. The crawling stopped and formed into the shape of fingers, then a hand on me. I froze. The hairs on my arm and the back of my neck stood up. Someone is touching me. I feel someone on me. I bolted my eyes open, stood up as best as I could and looked around me. The girl on my team next to me was fast asleep. I looked at the man in the window seat and he was wide awake. He was staring out the window, then he turned to me and just stared at me. I didn't understand why this was happening. I didn't see anything. Why is my mind playing tricks on me?

For the last time, I re-tucked myself into my blanket, scooting as close to the girl on my team as possible. I felt awful thinking a man I didn't even know may have

Chapter 5 – Slip

accidentally brushed up against me, but it still caused me to want to be as far away from him as I could in this close space.

As I closed my eyes, the crawling started immediately. The crawling was different, like it wasn't a memory. It was not in my head, but I still decided to ignore it. I knew practicing and praying over sharing my testimony made me relive being sexually assaulted for three years. It made me relive every single time it happened, remember the blame I placed on myself, and how I felt so alone and so ashamed. It took me years to be able to speak out and say what happened. It took me even longer to accept it wasn't my fault. Lastly, even longer to truly believe and act out in faith how God would use the nightmare of three years for good. I knew my God could, though. With everything in me, I prayed that my all-powerful God would stop this feeling right now on the plane. Stop the crawling. Stop the memories. Allow me to sleep. Allow me to pray for the country I am about to go into. Allow me to pray for the people I would meet. Allow me to pray for those who live there and are going to be a continuous contact point for those who have never even heard the name, Jesus.

Forcing myself to ignore the crawling that turned into fingers that transformed into a hand, I tried to sleep. I knew God would take it away, but He wasn't. I opened my eyes, refusing to move yet another time and readjust. I looked around me and the girl next to me was still sound asleep. The man was still wide awake, nothing on his screen, just staring away from me. I closed my eyes, begging for the beautiful peace like a wave to wash over me again. Out of nowhere, I felt afraid, and all I wanted to do was leave. There was no crawling that turned into fingers. There was a hand

Chapter 5 – Slip

tracing my waistband and entering. I could feel a cold hand against my skin.

I knew then that this was not a memory, this is happening. The man next to me is hurting me. My entire world started to swirl in my mind as he just continued. I burst my eyes open and he still continued. I searched the aisles for a flight attendant... no one. I couldn't see anything. The plane was pitch black. I was turning into that little girl; helpless and alone. I was the girl that just wrote a full-blown book about how God could turn the evilest circumstances into good, how our all-powerful God can utilize the darkest skeletons in our closets to share His good news.

When I was a little girl, I would get so angry when I wouldn't get my way or while fighting with one of my siblings. So angry that I would cry. Not because I was sad, but I was just that angry. As he continued, rage boiled inside me and bubbled over. My rage bubbled over into a single tear to fall down my face. More than anything I wanted to hurt him. I wanted to grab an airline magazine and hit him and run. I knew I couldn't. I didn't know him. I didn't even know his first name.

My anger boiling inside me, I knew I couldn't hit him, I knew it wasn't right, and I didn't know how strong this man was. I wanted to scream, but what would he do? How would he respond? What could he do if I screamed? I couldn't scream. I begged with God, just right now, make him stop. I want him as far away from me as possible. In that moment, the single word that rushed across my brain was "run." In an instant, I opened my eyes, threw down my blanket, grabbed his crawling hand from beneath my clothes, and pushed it away from me. For a split second, I was

Chapter 5 – Slip

looking into his eyes. I crawled over the girl and told her I needed to go to the bathroom. I didn't know what to do. I ran to the back of the plane where I knew there was a bathroom from my walk earlier in the flight.

Immediately I burst into tears. Then I saw a light further back behind the bathroom. I found two flight attendants and continued to heave tears. I told them what happened. The questions started to pile on. I couldn't speak through my tears. Then, I remembered, "She is still there. The girl on my trip is still sitting there near him." I told the flight attendants and they immediately moved him. I cried and cried and cried. When they came back and told me she was safe, I begged to go home. I told them that I didn't want to be here anymore. Please let me leave, let me call my mom. I need my mom.

They held me and asked how old I was. "19 years old." Are you alone? "No, I'm with a group. We are all going to Southeast Asia." Do you have adult leaders? "Yes." I tried to help the two kind flight attendants find where my leaders were. I pointed out their names so they could find their seating assignment. They brought the leaders back, a man and his wife. I had to tell them again what had just happened. She tried to console me by touching my leg and I just jumped away from her. I didn't want to be touched. I didn't want to talk anymore, I just wanted my mom. I needed to be back safe again.

My sponsors tried to calm me down. Then I got the worst response in the world: "Are you sure?" Am I sure? Of course I'm sure. I had to remove his hand from my pants. I had to run away from him. I am sure. I am more than sure. I couldn't contain the tears again, still begging for my mom.

Chapter 5 – Slip

After I calmed some, I got the talk. The talk about how there are different forms of touching. "He could have just been asleep and accidentally touched you." I was frozen. All of the color left my face. All of the life in that moment seemed to be sucked from me. All I could whisper unconsciously out of my mouth was, "You don't believe me..." The hurt that delivered those words must have shaken him to the core. He tried to shift, shift to problem-solving. The man is removed. The flight attendants have told us that the police at our layover airport have been called. He tried to talk sense into me. He tried to explain to me how he couldn't tell me to press charges or not. He couldn't tell me what to do; I am an adult and need to make the decision for myself.

I was reminded to take into account the group, the purpose of the trip, and where we will be landing. He told me quite frankly that no one could stay with me, or the whole group would be placed off schedule and I would be left alone in a foreign country. The purpose of our trip is to share the love of Jesus and how He has changed our lives. If I press charges in a foreign country, I am allowing time to be taken away from that mission. Lastly, we are landing in a foreign country. We found out that the man was from Iran. I am from America. We are both foreigners in a foreign country once we land.

The leader allowed me time to sit and think and pray about what I was going to do. I couldn't get past how I felt like no one believed me except these two flight attendants. In a few hours I was going to land in a foreign country where I knew no one. I needed to make one of the biggest decisions of my life, without my best friend, my mom, guiding me along the way. I sat and tried to calm myself. They moved my female leader to sit with me and the other girl. The head

Chapter 5 – Slip

flight attendant told me she informed the pilot and that I would need to write a statement to the airline. I wrote out exactly what happened and signed my name. I gave it back to the lead flight attendant.

It was like I was frozen. I heard the girl next to me saying she was so, so sorry. She had no idea, she was asleep. I just told her there is nothing to be sorry for, there is no way she could have known, I'm just glad we are both okay. But I wasn't okay. That is just what hurt people say to console those around them.

Sitting there, I tried to use logic to sort out my decision. I didn't want to fall headfirst into my emotions instead of leading with logic. Then I just started to cry. Why am I trying to solve this on my own? I felt like I was crying at the feet of Jesus, begging to know what to do because I couldn't do this on my own.

I knew in that moment the reason why I longed for my mom so badly is because she always turns me to the Bible. She always shifts my focus back to what God has planned for me. I needed to steer myself to Him on my own. Ask to know what to do.

Instantly, I got a wave of peace. The same wave I was begging for earlier. There was a whisper in the freshly silent airplane, "Vengeance is mine." I knew immediately. I got my answer. No. No, do not press charges. Do not stay in this foreign country and fight for yourself. Let me fight for you, Jillian. This isn't your battle to fight. My eternal father, the King of Kings, the Great I Am that I sing about in my car or on a Sunday morning, was telling me that He had everything under control. I don't have to rely on my power. God is

Chapter 5 – Slip

taking this load from my hands and dealing with my struggles for me. And I knew I wasn't strong enough, too.

Sitting there in the dark, quiet plane, I tried to sleep. Despite the fact I knew I was safe now, my heart was shaken. I was running through all of these thoughts in my mind when the lead flight attendant came up to me. She came to the aisle to discuss how we were to land. She wanted to tell me that when the plane lands, they will say a situation happened during the flight and for everyone to remain seated. Then, they will escort me and one sponsor off the plane with the man who hurt me.

Looking into her eyes, I saw that she was sorry. It was like her eyes apologized over and over without her mouth ever speaking the words. She continued to explain what would happen when we landed. Then, she asked me the golden question, "Will you be pressing charges?" I had to look into those eyes that seemed so upset for me, and say, "No, I won't be."

Her facial expression turned from sadness to great concern. She started to tell me that it was my decision, but my statement that I wrote for the airline tells a different story. It tells a story of needing to press charges. I had to look at her and say that I still wouldn't be pressing charges. She said okay, but the law enforcement on the ground was already contacted and I would need to tell them the same thing. She reassuringly brushed my shoulder and walked away.

I sat there for a split second, letting my mind take control of everything. I thought how I couldn't press charges because I believed that I'm not supposed to. Why does

Chapter 5 – Slip

'vengeance is mine' keep ringing in my ears? But... what about the other women? My mind went into the mode of a protector, longing to protect every other woman that this could happen to on an international flight, thinking of every person that has ever been impacted by sexual assault. I got so angry that my angry tears started to bubble inside me again and fall down my face. Finally, in an instant, I knew why. I knew why this happened. I thought back to how I struggled with shame, guilt, self-hatred, and so many other emotions when I had to go through the nightmare for three years of a man hurting me. Now older, a little smarter, and supposed to be stronger, God revealed it to me. I prayed. I prayed and I was watching a spiritual battle take place. Not just watching it, but fighting in it. Satan wanted to distract me. Satan wanted to break me, and turn me back around to go back to Texas.

Then, a light whisper entered my mind, "I let him." I let him? You let him? I sat there pouting, throwing myself the biggest pity party the plane could allow for in that seat, thinking, "Why, God, would you allow this to happen?"

The story of Job popped into my mind. If you don't know who that is or haven't heard his name in a while, he was a godly man in the Old Testament of the Bible. Personally, when I jump into a story, I like to have a little background knowledge on what is happening. It is like when my mom finds a new amazing Netflix show and I want to join in on the show. She has to stop and give me a verbal flowchart of all of the characters so that I am all caught up. I'm going to do that for you real quick.

Job had a beautiful family: a wife, sons, and daughters. In our day, we would consider him to be very

Chapter 5 – Slip

well-off. Back then, his wealth was represented by his livestock and his servants. Then, satan came to God and asked to test Job. Satan had the audacity to tell God that the only reason that Job is serving Him and loves Him is due to his great life. Well, God allowed for satan to change Job's circumstances but did not allow satan to touch Job himself. A servant then came to Job and told him how all his livestock was raided. Then another came to say how all his servants were killed along with more livestock. Lastly, a servant came to tell him that his sons and daughters were gathered when their house collapsed, and all of his sons and daughters have passed away.

Now, Job is known as a godly man, not only by his faith but his responses to each situation in life. When he had everything, Job praised God. Job lost all of his sons and daughters as well as most of his servants and livestock, all in one day. He weeps, but continues to praise God. Job praises the God who gives and takes away. Sitting here, I am amazed at that type of love. In our time, his situation would be equivalent to his whole family passing away except his wife, losing all his wealth, and job, all in one swoop. Despite it all, Job praises God.

We are fighting for our lives, and nothing makes satan more angry than when we walk out of the battle hurt and in pieces, but crawling right back to our eternal Father. Satan gets so upset because he knows that God is the only one in this entire universe who can mend the pieces back together again. Well, satan is no pushover, so he comes back again.

Now, all of the above just happens in the first chapter of Job! Whoever says the Bible is boring is sadly

Chapter 5 – Slip

mistaken. The Bible talks of God's divine creation, our fall, a lot of broken people choosing to love and live their lives to serve the King of Kings, our gift in Jesus Christ, His life, death, resurrection, the story of his life passed down through his apostles, and the revelation from God. I want to jump into Job 2:1-6, where we see how persistent satan really is. "One day the sons of God came again to present themselves before the Lord, and satan came with them to present himself before the Lord. The Lord asked Satan, "Where have you come from?" "From roaming through the earth," Satan answered Him, "and walking around on it." Then the Lord said to Satan, "Have you considered my servant Job? No one else on earth is like him, a man of perfect integrity, who fears God and turns away from evil. He still retains his integrity, even though you incited Me against him, to destroy him without just cause." "Skin for skin!" Satan answered the Lord, "A man will give up everything he owns in exchange for his own life. But stretch out Your hand and strike his flesh and bones, and he will surely curse You to Your face." "Very well," the Lord told Satan, "he is in your power; only spare his life."

Reading over the book of Job, which I suggest everyone should do, I realized so many lessons just in these six verses. Once I got to my hotel room, I remember facetiming my mom across the world. I was so broken trying to explain what happened. I was trying to somehow allow myself to speak out what had happened that seemed to be minutes ago in my mind. I could still feel him crawling on me. I just cried and cried. I remember my mom prayed over me and then I had to go. I needed to go to prepare for the day. But most importantly, I needed to dive into Scripture, so I started to read passages of Job, the Job that was stuck in my mind since the first plane ride.

Chapter 5 – Slip

Reading over God's word, I let myself declare God's truths over my life. I am a daughter of the Most-High King. God will never leave me or forsake me. Lastly, satan has no power. This last one amazes me because I can still remember running through my grandma's backyard and completely ruining some of her flowers in her flower bed. She brought me inside and asked me what made me do that? I had just learned about the bad guy that makes us do bad things named Satan, so I blamed him. I remember her face looking like she was trying not to laugh at me.

Looking back at the memory, I think she may have been holding back laughter because I did not fully understand the concept of satan yet. I didn't understand that he wasn't some evil villain in a cartoon. He wasn't this ugly, awful creature. Satan was an angel, so beautiful and so compelling that he took one-third of the angels with him to hell when God threw them out of heaven. Satan, although compellingly dangerous, has no power. The guy that seemed to tear apart the world has to go to the God we love for permission to interrupt our lives. Satan had to ask permission to test Job.

If you go back and look closely at those six verses like I did that day, you'll realize that God had so much confidence in Job that God suggested Job to Satan. I think of this moment and I think of how people have the saying that, "God gives His toughest battles to his strongest soldiers." I used to love that saying, but now I don't believe it to be true. Not one of us is more "tough" than another. God just knows how much each of us can handle while leaning and trusting in Him. In this moment in Scripture, it is like God has handpicked Job to suffer, not out of hatred or spite, but because God has full faith that Job will continue

Chapter 5 – Slip

to rely on Him. Closing my Bible across the world from my family, I realized that God said yes to Satan. God allowed satan to let this man hurt me. God gave permission for satan to place me in a battle that destroyed me once before.

In some ways, I thought this was too cruel to be true. In others, I believe God was and is trying to teach me something. When I was a little girl, I suffered through being a victim for three years. I struggled with the labels of "victim" and who everyone said I would become. I struggled with feeling like my life was taken away from me a little bit more each time. I had so much self-hatred, guilt, and shame. I felt like I had no one. I was completely secluded and eaten up inside. It took me years to finally realize how God could use that for good. It took me years to listen and see God's meaning.

When I was so young, I believe my healing took me so long because I didn't believe in Jesus. No part of me wanted to buy into the story of Jesus Christ. I struggled for so long and had to go through such a hard period in my life, even after it was reported and supposedly "over," because I was still fighting a raging battle within in me.

This time, about ten years later, my spiritual turnover time was much shorter. The healing is still in process, but the time it took for me to realize I needed to be renewed by God was instantaneous. That is nothing for me to brag about, nothing for me to shine the light of how much stronger, smarter, or how much more of, however many qualities that I am about ten years later. It has nothing to do with that. It has everything to do with my relationship with Jesus Christ.

Chapter 5 – Slip

I think of when people suffer who don't believe in Jesus and it burdens me to the core of my being because I don't know and will never fully understand their exact situation. But I have now seen in my life the pain and hurt that I've gone through. I see how I fought for so long by myself and the damage that I did to myself trying to fight the battle within me by myself. Now, as a believer in Jesus, it was a different story. Did I cry? Yes. Was I angry? Yes. Did I want to hurt him and fight him? Yes. Did I wonder why a random man on an airline would make the decision to hurt a stranger? Yes. Do I regret freezing? Yes. Was I hurt? Yes. Did I have nightmares for months afterwards? Yes. The pain did not lessen. The impact was not numbed, but my response drastically changed.

I turned to my Heavenly Father and sat on my hotel bed across the world from my family and friends, and I cried. I let every tear fall at the feet of Jesus. I begged Him for it to hurt less. For me to be able to have the reassurance that I did the right thing. I begged for Him to allow me to have a peace of mind. I begged Him to not let me spiral down like I did years before. I prayed and pleaded, "Don't let me become so angry that I try to leave You…"

At my weakest and in the midst of my hurt I realized that I was already doing better. I had reported immediately. That is a win, by the power of Christ. I was able to tell my mom and my family. That is a win, by the power of Christ. I was able to yell, scream, and cry at the feet of Jesus. That is a huge win, because I went to Him, all by the POWER of Christ. I opened my Bible to hear from God's living and active word about how He would still use me after the pain and hurt that was such a fresh, open wound. That is a win.

Chapter 5 – Slip

God allowed me to be placed in a position where I was truly a vessel to share my testimony and the good news with people across the world. God allowed me and said yes to me being in a situation where I knew I had no power BUT God. On my own, I would be on the next flight back home, crying in my family's arms. In my own power, I might have been trying to get the guts to yell and scream in the face of a stranger whose face I will never forget. By my own power, I would have fallen into a million pieces.

BUT God. For all my grammar people out there, it might drive you wild that one of my favorite sayings is "BUT God." It may not be grammatically correct, but it is more than correct spiritually in my life and in the Bible. Everything happens in our lives for a specific reason and to be used for the glory of God. I was shaken to my core by being placed in a spiritual battle on that airplane, BUT God equipped me with the full armor of God to fight and carry on. I wanted to end the mission trip for myself and go home, BUT God had a different plan by allowing me to form friendships and relationships with people I will never forget. God allowed me to tell my testimony and the gospel without hesitation or fear. God allowed me to see people hear Jesus' name for the very first time. He allowed me to minister to people who had heard His name and were ready to accept Jesus into their lives, and start living in a way to glorify God. If I wasn't a Christian, I would not have been able to even keep the pieces together. God placed me together like new and allowed me to continue to serve Him. I realize that this is a testimony in itself.

I realize that satan knew that I went into this trip without fear with an eternal peace that is only given by God. Satan knew that the only thing that he could use to shake me

Chapter 5 – Slip

to my core was to allow someone to sexually assault me. It was the thing that made me turn away from God for years. It was the hurt of being a victim that I believed a good God would never allow. It was all my compounded hurt and shame that made me turn away for so long. By the grace of God, I became a Christian. By the grace and power of God, satan tried and failed. I was hurt and felt guilt and shame, but this time I clung to God tighter than ever. I grabbed ahold of God like He was air in my lungs. I knew I couldn't move or make it without Him. I was angry and hurt, but I knew that by God's power I would be okay. He would restore my heart. God would allow this battle to be won and for me to be able to encourage people through it.

As a little kid, I never really did want to learn about all past wars and battles. I didn't want to hear about the victories or casualties. It hurt me too much to think of all the lives lost. Memorizing the dates instead of the stories became a challenge for me. Now, I realize it is important to learn about history so that we recognize where we have come from because we learn from our past responses. As a little girl without Christ, I turned away from Him and tried to fight on my own. Now older, I ran towards Christ and the healing is completely different. I pray that I continue to learn from my own past, other's testimonies, and rely on the strength of Jesus Christ within in me. Most importantly, I pray that I will hold onto the Bible like it is the air I breathe because God is the only one that will guide me in a battle and He is the only one that helped me through each day since I was sexually assaulted again. It is by His power that I can share and pray that others will use their healing or healed hurt to share the power of Christ in their weakest times.

Chapter 5 – Slip

I recognize that this incident on the plane was where I slid down the mountain. I did not break. I was not crushed, but I had a few scrapes and bruises to remember it by. I still needed healing, but I got back up and followed God's plan for me. In 2 Corinthians 4:7-9, Paul writes "But we, have this treasure in jars of clay, to show that the surpassing power belongs to God and not to us. We are afflicted in every way, but not crushed; perplexed, but not driven to despair, persecuted, but not forsaken; struck down, but now destroyed." The verse before this passage verse 6 pinpoints that the "treasure in jars of clay" is the knowledge of the glory of God. I know that I know that I know that I know, that God is sovereign. I know that by His redeeming love I am not driven to despair or crushed by what has happened to me because my God has a bigger plan for my life than what has happened to me. Every event and circumstance will be used to further the glory of God. Even in my weakest, God is strong. He is allowing me to be renewed each day. Reading this Bible passage allows me to realize that I am powerfully weak. That is who we are called to be as Christians. We are not meant to carry the burden of our lives on our own, but to give it to the Lord. We do not rely on our strength but on the power of Christ in us. And one day through the healing and after the hurt, God will turn our pain to praise.

Chapter 6

Step by Step

After I finally put my pain and fear aside from sliding down the mountain, we continued on as if nothing had just happened. Same pace. Same everything, just the memory of my slide was enough for me to grip onto the mountain a little harder with each crawl. Looking down, I tried to judge where we were. I thought we must be at least halfway, if not closer. I just knew that we were so close to the top. I started to crawl right behind my leader. Now it was just us two. We were quiet as we crawled, but he would let out a few warnings like, "Watch out for this rock, it's not stable," or, "Don't step right there, it's slippery from melted snow." I would just listen to his instructions and act. I didn't think anything of following after him because he knew about mountains and I didn't. I knew nothing.

My breathing began to be super heavy and I started to feel light-headed. I asked if we could stop. The leader stopped. He just stared at me as I took a swig from my water bottle and tried to catch my breath. I looked down and up, trying to figure out where we were. By this point, every muscle in my body ached. My feet hurt from walking for so long. My arms and back were stinging from all of the crawling. Muscles that I didn't even know I had were crying for me to stop. My bruises and scrapes were pleading for my attention. So I looked up to my leader, and said, "You can go to the top without me and I'll just wait right here." My leader looked at me and simply said, "No." I was very

Chapter 5 – Step by Step

surprised that he would just look at me and tell me I couldn't do something, especially an activity that is optional and taking such a bearing on my body. I looked back at him and didn't know how to respond. I think he knew that I didn't know how to respond because then he continued to say, "No, I believe you can. I refuse to let you stop now when you are this close." I continued to just try and catch my breath as I thought over what he said.

Most of the time in life, we have this false notion in our minds that God can't say no to us. The all-powerful God of the universe can't say 'no' to us, His creation. Taking a step back and looking at this opinion in the light seems laughable, but not when we are sinking deep.

There was a time in my life where I realized that I was broken and bruised, and no part of me wanted to continue on. Actually, if I'm honest, there are multiple times in my life that I have felt this way. I chose to look at my suffering as an option. If I started to hurt, I wanted to stop. I never understood the "good spiritual pain."

I am a dancer. I started dancing as a little girl in ballet like so many other girls, but I fell in love with it. I even learned how to tie my shoes by tying the little bow at the top of my ballet slippers.

One day, when I was about seven years old, I was dancing in the den of my grandmother's house to worship music. All of a sudden something in my heart just clicked and the joy of the songs made sense to me. My mom saw this and immediately wanted to get me back into dancing.

Chapter 5 – Step by Step

Later on, I was able to be a part of the praise dance team at Oak Cliff Bible Fellowship. I remember after one practice I rushed up to my mommy and I was just so happy. I had found out that I would be near the front of the stage and then in the aisles for the Easter service. I was most excited that I would get to go down to the aisles because then I could be dancing close to people. It was weird to love the people in the audience not to get applause at the end, but simply to tell them of God's love with no words. Your body is telling the story of Christ's redeeming love, the peace He gives, and His power that will never fail. I couldn't contain my joy because I knew it was my avenue to share Christ with people.

Well, on that Easter Sunday I danced and I heard nothing. Nothing at all. It seemed to be complete silence, but as I was dancing I had goosebumps the entire time. It wasn't that it was cold, but more like the presence of the Lord rushed over me. It was just God and me, and I was praising Him with my every movement and my every step.

In that simple dance, I could feel the closeness that I experienced with God. I was willing for God to take over all of me and be in that intimate moment with me. As we get older, we get a little more prone to fighting off still, quiet, all-encompassing moments with the Lord. I thought I was serving through dance, and I was. Most importantly it was my form of worship to honor the Lord.

An important component in dancing is stretching. As a dancer, I learned early on that there is a good hurt and a bad hurt. The good hurt is where you are stretching yourself to the point of becoming more flexible, so next time you can do better on your leaps. There is also a bad hurt,

Chapter 5 – Step by Step

though. The bad hurt is where you have pushed yourself too far. You have pushed yourself past the point of stretching and into the position of an injury.

I believe as Christians today we don't want any type of hurt. We don't want good hurt or bad hurt. We all have a yearning to go through life with as much ease and comfort as possible. I refuse to lie to you, so here is the truth: in John 15:19 Jesus says, "If you were of the world, the world would love you as its own; but because you are not of the world, but I chose you out of the world, therefore the world hates you." Jesus is being blunt about how, as Christians, we will be persecuted. We will be uncomfortable. We will feel out of place. We know and feel all of these things because our citizenship is not of this earth. Our citizenship relies in Heaven. (Philippians 3:20).

While we are seeking how to make the Christian walk the most convenient in our lives, God wants to stretch us and mold us. Unfortunately, we don't want the pressure placed upon us because it is too much for us to handle. Actually, that is right. It is too much for us to handle. God has placed us in such a way that we need to rely on Him.

On our own, we can only go so far before the bad hurt starts to set in, the bad hurt of going past where we were supposed to go. The pain from not relying fully and truly on our Savior God to take care of our current situation.

We have another option, though. We can choose to stretch. We can choose to rely on God fully in a way that He orchestrates each of our footsteps. We can rely on Him so much that we can see vividly where He wants us to go in accordance with our life.

Chapter 5 – Step by Step

There was a time after my incident on the plane where I believed that it was a bad hurt. I started to question God's sovereignty and His will. Why did He allow me to step foot onto a plane where He knew it would shake me? Why? Why wouldn't He allow me to just not raise enough funds? Why wouldn't God stop him? Why?

I couldn't think about what happened without tears rolling down my face. I couldn't open my mouth to cry out to God without bitterly crying out, "Why?" My pain seemed to be more than I could bear. The world named it compound trauma, but it was something else. It was something much deeper than that.

I went through a time period when I got back from my mission trip, where I tried to pretend it was all a nightmare. I pretended nothing had happened and I could move on with my life. However, it was like I couldn't move on and I couldn't fall back into my normal routine because it still haunted me.

I didn't pray because all I could mutter was, "Why?" But I continued to go to church. I continued to meet with people who poured Scripture into me. God continually and intentionally placed me in situations where I could be spiritually filled.

I have heard time and time again in the church that we need to be poured into. We need to be poured into by a spiritual mentor and we need to be pouring out into others by helping to disciple and hold others accountable to God's word. At this time in my life, I felt like I was being poured into so much, but my cup was not overflowing. It was like Satan had asked to have permission to cut a slit in my cup

Chapter 5 – Step by Step

and God said yes. It was like there was a leak, and when I thought I was doing better and tried to pour out and continue in fellowship, I would find myself empty more quickly than I would find myself full.

Then one night, I broke. Out of all the places this could have happened, I was in the shower. The memories started to come rushing back until it was like a flood in my brain. I could do nothing but fall to my knees and cry.

Then I remembered John 11:35, the shortest verse in the Bible: "Jesus wept." I never understood in the Bible when it highlighted that "Jesus wept." But it shows how Jesus was fully divine and fully human at the same time. As I was crying so hard it seemed I could barely breathe. I kept crying and crying and I could feel the water beating over me. In that still, quiet moment where all I could hear were my own sobs, it was like Jesus was crying, too. It was like the water washing over me was no longer the shower, but with my eyes closed sobbing, it was like my Heavenly Father crying with me. His tears were washing over me and healing me of all my hurt.

The tears running over me was when I realized I was being stretched. I would not be pulled till the breaking point, but God would turn my pain to praise. I started to actively pray. At first, all I could focus my prayer on was my healing, and my strength, and my joy, and my will to continue to follow Jesus Christ. Then, I finally uttered the words, and I barely realized they came out of me, "I forgive him."

It was like the biggest exhale in the world; the decision to move on. The forgiveness granted to the one who had chosen to steal something from me. I forgive him...

Chapter 5 – Step by Step

The man from Iran that I will probably never see again. The face that is burned into my memory forever. The man who chose to hurt me, a total stranger on the plane. I forgive you.

Suddenly, I started to pray to forgive everyone that had ever hurt me. I prayed for everyone that I had ever wronged. I prayed slowly for each person and prayed for each of us, including myself, to have a heart change. God was turning my pain to praise.

Coming out of that shower, it seemed like I was a whole new woman. I couldn't think to say anything but "thank you." Thank you God for taking this weight off of me. It was bearing me down. You brought me back up. I couldn't help but laugh because I know many people close to me will sit in a bath to destress or shower to calm themselves down, but this was so much different. God had intervened on my behalf and wept with me. He cleansed me of my hurt and was showing me that I would be okay. I was not fully okay in that moment, but I was refreshed. I was thankful for the weight taken from me. I was glad that the King of Kings was on my side and that He had given me the power to forgive.

I don't want to skim over that like it is something easy to do. Forgiveness is not something you can put on your list of to-do's one day. It is a process and it is painful, but it is so worth it. Hurt holds people captive. Hurt can place us in bondage and we can get so used to functioning with it that we will barely notice that it is there. I think this is sad, but I have been in that position before. I have laid in my unforgiving heart so long that I knew how to live with it. The difference after truly forgiving those that moment in the shower is that it is a continual daily choice.

Chapter 5 – Step by Step

I decided to give up my right to hurt you for hurting me. One more time, give up the right to hurt them for hurting you. That is when you realize God is making this a good hurt. He is stretching you so that you will be able to better serve His kingdom. He allowed Satan to test you in such a way it hurt, but one day your testimony will give God's kingdom glory. People will see your wounded heart being healed from the inside out. Your pain is being turned into praise. In 2 Corinthians 4:16-18 Paul writes "So we do not lose heart. Though our outer self is wasting away, our inner self is being renewed day by day. For this light momentary affliction is preparing for us and eternal weight of glory beyond all comparison, as we look not to the things that are seen but to the things that are unseen. For things that are seen are transient, but the things that are unseen are eternal." We may not see right in this moment why God is allowing pain to enter our lives. We may not understand why we had to suffer the way we did. The promise that is given to us as Christians is that our situation will be used for the eternal weight of glory. We may not see it now, today, or tomorrow. You may be blessed with the opportunity for some of the pieces to fit together to get a glimpse of what God's reasoning is. Either way, find peace in the fact that God has intervened in your story to transform you and others into something beautiful.

After that moment of choosing to forgive, I have continually decided to take off my bondage. An unforgiving spirit will not take hold of me. I have released them from any debt in my eyes. Now, I am living better because of it. It is like my bruises started to fade and my muscles have started to relax. The soreness that used to be so fresh is now a memory to strive me forward. So I will keep going forward to the mission God has placed on my life, in complete

Chapter 5 – Step by Step

freedom, despite the pain that I have been through. I continue to stay in an intimate relationship with God. Our trials and our pain are not meant to push us away from God the Father. They are meant for us to grow in a more intimate relationship with Him and grow in such a way where we can continue on stronger than we were before. Continue forward with a memory of how God provided and delivered us in our time of need. How the Lord washed us clean despite us running away time and time again. God had healed my hurt, and He can heal yours too.

Your situation in life should never drown out your vision of God and His plan for your life.

Chapter 5 – Step by Step

Chapter 7

Peak

After resting and reflecting on his words, I just started to gaze up towards the peak. Then my eyes retraced my climb and I thought of all of the beauty surrounding me. A deep breath in and then a deep breath out. Wow, I have come a long way. I had to be three-quarters of the way done now. I knew it.

Instead of this forming encouragement inside me, it ended up pacifying me. I thought, "I didn't make it to the top this time but look how far I have come. That is an accomplishment in itself." After that thought rushed before the forefront of my brain, I knew my thinking was incorrect. I was allowing myself to give up but give myself a big pat on the back for trying. Trying isn't good enough.

Finally, after much persuasion from the guide and internal debate, I got up. Every muscle in my body cried "why?" but at this point I had decided that I would reach the peak. When I was younger, I remember going to a summer camp put on by my school's athletic department. It was called strengthening and conditioning camp. On those blistering hot days where I just wanted to eat ice cream and watch TV, I was outside running laps and lifting. All of the students there were athletes trying to stay in shape for their sport. The coaches would yell for us to remember mind over matter as sweat beaded down our foreheads. I always thought it was such a weird saying to think your mind could

Chapter 7 – Peak

control how far you could go. Years later on the side of a mountain, I knew exactly why that coach used to yell mind over matter. My whole body was telling me "no," but my mind knew I needed to reach the top.

As I continued to fall in step behind the guide, I looked up past him and all I could see for the first time was blue. The alluring blue skies above us looked so close that I wanted to reach out and touch it. I kept looking towards what I knew would be the end, and finally, I took the last step. We made it to the peak!

It still doesn't make sense to me how exhausted and unbelievably tired I felt on the way up the mountain, but right when I climbed over the edge to stand up on the peak, everything changed. My heart felt like it was pounding outside of my chest. I stood confidently on top of the mountain and my whole body had butterflies. The initial rush of energy that evaporated during the climb was found once again inside of me. Looking out onto the horizon of the beautiful mountains surrounding ours, I was so thankful that my leader forced me to keep going.

Standing at the peak, I slowly turned around, trying to soak in every inch of God's creation. Let me tell you, I didn't think it could get any more beautiful, but it did. I was so high up that everything below looked tiny.

Then, my leader told me to soak it up some more. I was allowing the experience to wash over me, praising the Lord for how beautifully He made each and every living thing. The clouds were like marshmallows sitting in the sky. All the colors of the world were more vibrant than ever

Chapter 7 – Peak

before. It was like I got a new lens on life once I reached the peak. I could see the world more clearly now.

Then, the guide told me I could take a rock from the top to keep. So I looked and found one that seemed to sparkle. A victory rock. A rock of the testimony that I made it. I was not even close to being prepared for the next words from the guide: we would need to head back down. Down? Why would I ever want to go back down? This is amazing! I love this moment! I want to stay here in this moment in awe of God's presence.

Besides the Rocky Mountains and the ocean, the smallest I have ever felt in life is in New York City. There are skyscrapers sitting so tall that you have to lean back to see where the top of the buildings kiss the sky. I strain my little neck all the way back and I am still not able to see past all of the shining lights and all of the billboards. Times Square. New York City. The hustle and bustle that makes you feel like you are not doing enough in your own life because you don't understand the sense of urgency that everyone around you is feeling.

At five years old, my mom and my grandma brought all of us to New York City. We were there for the Macy's Thanksgiving Day parade. Y'all know it! It's the parade with the floating balloons in the shape of characters that take up blocks at a time due to their size. We watched from inside a restaurant and were mesmerized by all the people standing around the streets watching the parade. We were amazed at the number of people underneath one big balloon character that was floating through the city and perplexed as to why

Chapter 7 – Peak

that many people have to hold up something that should be seemingly light to carry.

When the parade was over and Santa had passed by, the thousands of people started to go back to their own lives. For one point in time, we were all synced and focused on the same thing, but now we have to go back to our own lives. My mom and grandma got us up from watching within the restaurant and grabbed ahold of each of our hands.

If you didn't know, I am one of four children. I have an older brother, older sister, and a younger brother. My grandma held tightly onto two of my siblings' hands, and my mom held mine and my other sibling. Right when we passed the doors back onto the sidewalk, the holding hands turned into a white-knuckle grip. The kind of grip when you hold on to something so tight you see your hand is not the same color anymore. This is the grip my mom had on me. We started walking and the crowds of people started to engulf me.

I was so little that when people started to flood the sidewalk next to us, I saw my mom starting to fade. The more people started to surround me, the more I could no longer see my mom. I was lost in New York City. I felt the pressure of people surrounding me moving me forward, but not being able to see my mom struck a chord in me that could never be forgotten. I panicked. I let out a blood-curdling scream. I kept screaming and screaming. Shrieking with no words. Yelling out for my mom. Nothing. No response. All I could feel was this pressure of people still moving me forward.

Chapter 7 – Peak

Then, all of a sudden, I felt a squeeze. A squeeze on the hand I had elevated in front of me all along. A yank with such force that I ran into my mom again. I was back right next to her. Tears streaming down my face, panic starting to cease. I could see my mom clearly.

Now, I can look back and laugh with my mom about the fear that I had. She had never let go of my hand, and I was never ever lost. I just lost sight of her and panic set in. My mind couldn't understand that she was still there if I couldn't see her.

I believe this is exactly how we are with Jesus. I believe that God is guiding us through life, but when circumstances start to pile on and surround us, we refuse to search for Him. We feel so tired and so small that we assume that we are all alone. Without a doubt in our minds, we have no one to help us. We lash out at God, we cry, beg, and scream at Him. Then, when all of our situations fade, and when life slows down some more, we can see Him again. Our security is back.

Why couldn't we have just seen Him before? Why did I go into such a panic when I could no longer see my mom guiding me? Why, when we see our comfort, do all of our anxieties wash away? We are afraid of the unseen. We find comfort in the known. We like to see what is going on because if we can see it happening in our minds, we mistake that as being given some form of control.

When I was battling inside myself whether to continue up the mountain or not, I wasn't certain where on my journey I was. I was battling with the uncertainty and the unseen. When the things that are unseen creep into the

Chapter 7 – Peak

picture, panic starts to burn inside of us. Hebrews 11:1 says, "Now faith is the assurance of things hoped for, the conviction of things not seen." Before I ever took a step towards the mountain and before I even got into the car that day, I had a hope to complete the journey at the peak of a mountain. I knew that was the final destination that I was striving for. The problem became during the journey when the conditions weren't what I expected, and everything didn't go as I planned, so I no longer wanted to continue on.

So many times in our lives, if things don't go the way we plan or the conditions of our life aren't what we want, we see it as a disaster. We are set into a state of confusion, no longer able to see the whole picture or the end goal. The control we had over every part of our lives was revealed as an illusion and we don't know how to handle it. We had an illusion of control the whole time.

How do we deal with that? Well, we should have faith in God that surpasses things that we can see. We can't see God working on our behalf all the time, but He is. We can't see our finish line when we start a race, but it is there. I couldn't see the peak when I was going over its edge, but I made it.

Celebrate the decision to carry on. Not getting swallowed up by the busyness and immediacy of this world is a task that all Christians have to fight. We need to praise God in the process. I was so busy complaining about my pain, how I slid, and how I wanted to stop, that I didn't get to soak in the whole experience as much as I could have. I got lost in my surroundings. Just like when I was a little girl having my mom tightly gripping my hand in New York City the whole time, I was distracted by the flood of people

Chapter 7 – Peak

surrounding me. Your situation in life should never drown out your vision of God and His plan for your life. One more time. Your current state that you are in should not distract you from what God has called you to do and to be.

God is bringing you through a journey in life. Sometimes we are going through valleys and other times we are climbing mountains. Wherever we are, God is there also. God says in Isaiah 41:10 "Fear not, for I am with you; be not dismayed, for I am your God; I will strengthen you, I will help you, I will uphold you with my righteous hand." God is with us in the beginning, during the process, and in the victory. We need to learn to soak up the process just as much as we treasure the end. God's hand and power are with us all along; we need to act like it.

The short time I spent at the peak of the mountain was only a fraction of the time that I spent climbing the mountain. Don't get me wrong, it was rewarding. The victory of conquering the climb felt amazing.

The thing is, God has called us to follow Him, and we cannot live off of the few highs that we have in this life. We can't live off of Christian conferences. We can't live off of Sunday morning church. We can't live off of worship music in the car. We need to be completely saturated in God's word to the point that the word of God flows from you just like the words from your mouth. When you are flourishing your relationship with Christ, you can see how every waking minute of your life has a purpose. Not just Sunday mornings. Not just mission trips. Not just conferences. The entire journey of your life is to be completely surrendered to God. The journey that God has called us on is worth it. Each person God has placed in our life is worth it. The school and job we are at is our mission field. Treasure each step of the way as much as we adore the peaks in our lives, and let God do the rest.

God is bringing you through a journey in life. Sometimes we are going through valleys and other times we are climbing mountains.

CHAPTER 8

Descend

After a little while longer, reality did set in. I knew that I would have to go down. I squeezed my small sparkling rock from the top of the mountain so that I could remember this moment. I wanted to remember every part of the experience exactly how it was. Clutching the rock in my hand a little harder, I took one more look around me. I was ready to go.

I started to go down by myself, and my leader shouted, "Wait!" I looked back at him and he told me, "You still need to follow me, going down can be just as hard as going up sometimes." I always thought about the climb like walking downstairs. Up is the hardest part and walking down is a breeze.

For a little while, I felt silly. Of course, I would need to follow my leader. Yes, I made it to the top, but I still had never climbed down something as big as this before, and I didn't know how to go down on my own. He placed himself in front of me and explained that we would do kind of like a backwards crawl down the mountain. I would again need to carefully follow after his step.

Initially, going down seemed much easier than going up. I guess it had to do with my adrenaline pumping from reaching the peak, and it was easier to let my body just go down than it was to pull myself up. Well, right when I

Chapter 8 – Descend

stopped paying attention, I started to slip. My heart dropped, and my whole body immediately tensed. Looking around me I thought, "I am so thankful this was nothing like the slide coming up the mountain." My leader asked me worriedly "Are you okay?" I nodded yes, and I have no doubt that he could physically see that I was not as shaken as the first time. He responded "That's good. We have almost reached the bottom. Be careful and be aware of each of your steps."

As I continued down the mountain, I just stayed in awe of how God made everything so detailed. I was determined to soak in my surroundings this time. After my mini slide, I knew not to completely zone out into my surroundings, but there was a sense of joy that washed over me. I was drenched in a joy that only God can provide. A tingle of excitement from when God lets you in on one of His plans.

We finally reached the bottom and we met all of my friends there! I couldn't help but tell them about all I had experienced. The one girl that made it halfway told me, "I wish I would have kept going." That really hit hard for me. I wanted to quit, too. I wanted to quit with everything in me. I wanted to quit, but I didn't. Far enough wasn't good enough for me after the encouragement from the guide. I wanted to experience it all and I am glad that I was able to.

For my third semester of college, I transferred universities for multiple reasons. I struggled with finding my place and finding a new balance to my new life. I wanted to keep encouraging people with Jesus' love more than anything else in the world. It didn't take me long to realize that I was

Chapter 8 – Descend

in a battlefield. A constant battle. I felt like I was removed from a bubble into a war zone within a blink of an eye. At one instance, I was at a university that was pouring into me God's Word constantly. Then, I was pushed into the front lines. Every corner I turned something was against what I believed. Some didn't really know about Jesus, others could care less.

As I continued through my semester, I felt all the days slowly tearing away at me. It wasn't an awful school, it was the constantly defending my faith and being the sole person to stand up for what I believed in that became exhausting.

Each morning growing up, my mom would bring us down to the kitchen table and lead us in a morning devotional. I remember one time she said, "One day you will thirst for God's word, like your need for water." I never understood that. As a little girl, I was very confused, like mom, if we don't have water for three days we can die. What do you mean that the Bible is as vital as and actually more vital than water?

At my new university, I lived thirsty for God's word. I went from a university that would have Monday, Wednesday, and Friday chapel. I would go to Bible studies, mentor meetings, and church on Sundays. All of this on top of my daily devotional. I was soaking up the Lord and all that He had to teach me. Switching to my new university, I would wake up and I could not even brush my teeth before I sat at my desk and opened up my Bible. I could not continue throughout my day without hearing from God. I felt a deep yearning for Him like I never had before.

Chapter 8 – Descend

I am not saying this to promote private schools or colleges. I am addressing it because I lost my support system, I lost my church family and my spiritual mentors. It felt like the ground was taken right from under me. I thought I would be able to handle it better because I went to public schools all my life. I was never "sheltered" like some people may say. I didn't have the privilege of growing up with chapel or Bible courses. Although I did have the privilege of a mom that set the best possible example of how to follow God and surround yourself with a strong church family.

Dealing with a transition of schools and the incident on the plane became too much to bear on my shoulders. I lied to myself and told myself that I had completely surrendered it to God back in Southeast Asia. I was able to surrender everything to God and that is why I was able to continue on the mission trip. The truth being told, I laid it down for Jesus to handle and when I came back to the United States, I took it back upon myself. The very moment I took the burden back was at the baggage claim in the airport. I saw my mom entering the doors, and I ran over to her and I just broke down. All the tears were flowing. Looking back, I wonder what people were thinking, like, "Wow she really missed her mom" or "She was just homesick." In reality, I needed her. The person I was fully placing my trust in was God, but I was growing weary because I knew I needed my support system to hold me close to the Lord as well. I struggled with blaming myself. No one in the world can hug all the confusion and hurt out like a mama can. She just held me, and best of all, she kept pointing me to Christ. Keep running, running back to the feet of your unconditionally loving Savior.

Chapter 8 – Descend

The biggest difference being across the world and at my own campus was the fully trusting in God part. I went to a new university and all of a sudden all of the peace and trust that I was daily surrendering to the Lord was back on my shoulders. I had taken it back right after I had given it to Him. It was a daily surrender, until I stopped. Then, I couldn't hold it all. I broke.

At a point in the semester, I was trying to find a mentor and found an amazing woman. I tried to tell her my testimony, and I broke. I hadn't broken while telling my testimony since the first few times I said what I went through for three years out loud. She told me that it was going to be okay, and I knew it was. She told me she wanted me to meet another survivor and that may help me with being able to share my story.

In reality, I know why I was broken. I broke not because of those three years that I stayed silent. I broke down because I was a nineteen-year-old young woman that had just let someone do it again. I broke because the hurt was so raw, and no one wanted to press me. No one wanted the details of what happened, no one wanted to talk about different solutions, and no one wanted to check in on me. I don't blame anyone, I have a great support system. I just felt the people closest to me walking around on eggshells, so terrified of saying the wrong the thing that they limited themselves to saying nothing.

It didn't really matter much to me at first because I thought I had resolved it with God. Well, the funny thing about me is I tend to go back and grab what I give to Jesus. It is a constant struggle. If in my mind "God is taking too long," I want to go and speed up the process. It makes me

Chapter 8 – Descend

laugh because I have so many women in the Bible to look towards to know this is not the way. Yet I still take all of my baggage back and keep rolling it around with me, and all the while I am wondering why I am so tired.

    One of the prime examples I think of is Sarai. God promised her husband Abram descendants that would amount to the stars of the sky. If these names don't sound familiar to you, they are later named Sarah and Abraham in the Bible. Anyway, she knew that she wasn't able to have children, so she tried to run ahead of God and place everything in her own hands. In Genesis 16:1-6 the Bible says, "Abram's wife Sarai had not borne any children for him, but she owned an Egyptian slave named Hagar. Sarai said to Abram, "Since the Lord has prevented me from bearing children, go to my slave; perhaps through her I can build a family." And Abram agreed to what Sarai said. So Abram's wife Sarai took Hagar, her Egyptian slave, and gave her to her husband Abram as a wife for him. This happened after Abram had lived in the land of Canaan 10 years. He slept with Hagar, and she became pregnant. When she realized that she was pregnant, she treated her mistress with contempt. Then Sarai said to Abram, "You are responsible for my suffering! I put my slave in your arms, and ever since she saw that she was pregnant, she has treated me with contempt. May the Lord judge between me and you." Abram replied to Sarai, "Here, your slave is in your hands; do whatever you want with her." Then Sarai mistreated her so much that she ran away from her."

    One thing I love about the Bible is how honest it is. Sometimes if you are writing anything, you have to clean stuff up a bit for it to be "appropriate," but the Bible is true. It shows a realistic account of events. Sarai ran ahead of God,

Chapter 8 – Descend

and her slave became pregnant. Then, Sarai became pregnant. Now, with hormones raging, there are two pregnant women, and Sarai wants Hagar gone.

When I was younger, I never understood the concept of running ahead of God. I was so innocent in thinking, "Why can't people patiently wait for God to answer their prayers and provide?" A little older now, I can say it is because we don't trust Him. Let me take away that "we" because I don't want to group us all together, but I can testify to myself on multiple accounts. As a senior in high school, finding two tumors, one on each ovary, I wished more than anything in the world to have been a teen mom. It sounds crazy now! But then, in that moment, with the doctors asking if I really wanted to have kids, it made a lot of sense. What I was saying without realizing it is, "God, I don't trust you enough to handle all that is going on in my life, so I'm gonna try to run this one or wish I would have because I don't believe that You, the Creator of all things, can do the impossible." Do y'all hear how dumb I sound? But I struggle with doing this all the time, and I have to constantly and daily surrender my life to Christ. I constantly remind myself of who I could have become. I have to constantly remind myself of how it could have been so much worse without God on my side, and remember the never-changing and only important factor in the equation is Jesus Christ.

This point in my life where I would continually take back my pain, guilt, and shame was my minor slide on the way back down. I thought I had gotten past it. I even thought I was through the worst of it, but in reality, I had to learn how to live with what happened and that is an obstacle in itself. Yes, I survived the major slide, yes I was able to continue on and minister to the people in Southeast Asia, but

Chapter 8 – Descend

coming back home was when I slid again. Descending that mountain was the point where I was admiring how God got me through it, but not with my full heart. I wanted to run ahead of God. I wanted to tell Him how I wanted to deal with things and how long I wanted the healing process to last. I wanted to take back control right when I started to see familiar surroundings. Sarai from the Bible and I know that jumping ahead of God will result in a fall.

During my semester at the new college, I met with the girl that my newfound mentor wanted me to talk to. I went into the meeting thinking that I would be able to share Christ's love with her and see where she was in her walk with God and truly listen to her story. I got to the meeting and there was a total change of events. She told me what had happened, and I hurt for her. Sitting there with her flashed me back to interning at a women's safe house in Texas. I would sit and listen for hours of women's stories and my whole heart would break for them, and all I would want to do more than anything was help. I just wanted to reach out and help bring them out of the hole they were in, but I had to wait for when they were willing to come out. After talking with this girl for a while, I shared with her what happened when I was younger and what had happened just a few months prior, and in front of a complete stranger, I broke again. It was the first time after reporting it that I had told someone outside of my family what had happened. She had started to intern with children who were abused and wanted to go into a field of helping people who were sexually assaulted. She told me the reason I was hurting so bad was "compound trauma." I didn't fully understand what that meant, but when I calmed down, I realized that it was simple. I had hurt on top of hurt. It takes varying amounts of time for people to recover from multiple types of trauma, whether

Chapter 8 – Descend

that be sexual assault, serving in a war, or a car wreck. Talking with her, she encouraged me to press charges. She told me how I still had time to sue if I wanted to. I could get my revenge and allow him never to forget who I was.

Immediately, I thought that this was exactly what I needed. His face is burned into my mind, I want mine to be burned into his. I want him to admit to everyone what he did. I want to know more about him. I was in such a stage of wanting. Questions started to pop up into my head: "Who was this man? Yes, he was from Iran, but what does he do for a living? Does he have a family? Does he believe in God?" All of these questions kept swirling in my mind until I knew definitely in all of my willpower that I would sue.

That night, my brain wouldn't let me go to bed. I was tossing and turning and playing over and over in my mind the end of the flight. I was sitting by my female sponsor and the other girl. The airline said that they were going to have us escorted off of the plane first, but the announcement indicated there was an incident, and to remain seated. After remaining seated, a flight attendant walked up to my row and told me they were going to let everyone leave the flight and then they were going to bring the law enforcement onto the airline. I agreed and sat there. My male sponsor was a few rows forward, and he was going to stay with me. Sitting there watching everyone else leave, I started to regret my decision. I started to think I did want to press charges because I couldn't let this man get away with this. If he gets away with this today, then he will get away with it again and again. As everyone slowly filed out of the airplane moving on to their next destination, I was stuck. Stuck trying not to regret my decision across the world.

Chapter 8 – Descend

Then, men in white and the flight attendants came up to me. I remember that in a way, they seemed like angels walking down the aisle of the plane. I wondered where the law enforcement was, and quickly realized they were law enforcement. I stood next to my sponsor, and like a little girl searching for her parent's protection, I kept looking at him, trying to make sure that I was going to be okay. Like somehow, he could protect me if the man popped up out of nowhere.

The law enforcement took my statement from the lead flight attendant, and he read over it. He then looked at me as more of a statement than a question, "We are pressing charges today?" I let out a little whisper "No." "Excuse me, ma'am did you say no?" A little louder this time, "Yes, I do not want to press charges."

The law enforcement and the flight attendants surrounding me looked so puzzled. I wish I could say that I wasn't puzzled with myself as well, but in the moment, I decided I did not want to be in a foreign country by myself pressing charges, I couldn't do it. The other law enforcement man looked at me so kindly and said, "We will protect you, and we believe you. Right now, he is denying everything, but we have ways to make him admit it. All you need to do is to press charges." I looked down at the airplane carpet, and brought up from the pit of my stomach, "No." The last no hurt the worst. He denies everything. Everything that I knew more than the air I breathe to be true, he denies it all. He denies anything ever happened.

A tear fell down my cheek as they took my picture of my statement, my ticket, and passport for their records. The lead flight attendant held me so tight you would have

Chapter 8 – Descend

thought we were family. I stood there awkwardly. I didn't want to be touched. I didn't want anyone to touch me. But I appreciated her support. She had truly helped me through the entire process. They introduced me to a new flight attendant that was going to walk my sponsor and me to our next gate for our connecting flight.

As I continued down the aisle, she told me that the man was going to be on my left, and I didn't need to look if I didn't want to. As I walked down the aisle, I kept my eyes forward, and then unconsciously, I looked over to see his face one last time. He looked at me with no expression. No remorse, no anger, nothing. Then when we locked eyes, I could tell he knew I didn't press charges and he let out one deep laugh. I jerked my head back forward, his face and his single laugh burned into my memory. I realized at that moment that I meant nothing to him, and he knew that he had just won. He won because he hurt me. What hurt the most was knowing it meant nothing. He wasn't going to remember me, he wasn't even going to acknowledge what he did. He had just altered my life, and he was completely unfazed. Thinking of this, I could feel a lump in my throat growing, threatening to make me bawl. Threatening to make me break down in front of everyone, but I refused to. I just kept walking. I don't know his name, but I will forever remember his face. I will remember what he did, and it will haunt me. But by the power of God, I will get through this.

So when I was offered the opportunity for revenge months later, the sound of that was like music to my ears. I went back to my dorm that night and looked up as many attorneys in the area that would be able to take my case. I looked up criminal versus civil court. I looked up what to even charge him with. I spent hours pining over my

Chapter 8 – Descend

computer with so much hate in my heart. I was letting my anger take complete control of my actions, and I didn't even care in the least. I wanted to make him hurt. I wanted to make him pay.

I started to look up other women who were sexually assaulted on airplanes, trying to see what avenues they took. Then, I kept running into how they settled. They settled for a certain amount of money. At first, I thought, "You know what, that is good with me. You need to compensate me for what you put me through. I need something good to come out of this."

This anger search continued for days, which turned into weeks. Then, I found the attorney. I knew exactly who I was going to sue with. I knew exactly what to charge him with. He was one of the top sexual assault attorneys for many types of assault. I knew with almost every part of me that this was what I was going to do. I contacted the attorney, and I expected to have a peace within me, but I didn't. I felt nothing. The next morning, I was contacted by the attorney, and he told me that he would not take my case. I sat at my desk and tears just fell from my eyes. I sat there and just cried and cried. During the process, I tried to pretend like I was including God in all of my plans, when in reality, I was the driving force behind it all. I would send up a half-serious prayer saying that if He allowed me to find an attorney, it was God's will, but if not, then it wasn't. When I got the no, it shook me to the core. He told me I would need to find someone who specialized in international law.

Through my tears, I felt a huge warmth. I felt the calming peace that only God could provide, and I just sat there. I was still, trying to listen. I knew I had failed in my

Chapter 8 – Descend

eyes. I wanted to sue him, I wanted to get my revenge. Then, like a punch in the gut, the words came across my mind again, "Vengeance is mine."

Only then was I willing to open my Bible. Only when all of my efforts to get justice on my own failed did I sit still and listen to God. Only then did I look to see God's will. I opened my Bible reluctantly and turned to Romans 12:17-21 "Do not repay anyone evil for evil. Try to do what is honorable in everyone's eyes. If possible, on your part, live at peace with everyone. Friends, do not avenge yourselves; instead, leave room for His wrath. For it is written: Vengeance belongs to Me; I will repay, says the Lord. But if your enemy is hungry, feed him. If he is thirsty, give him something to drink. For in so doing you will be heaping fiery coals on his head. Do not be conquered by evil, but conquer evil with good."

I felt so hypocritical and stupid. I remember on the flight hearing, "vengeance is mine" and that is why I decided not to press charges, but when I got back to my home and a few people supported me pressing charges, I let it consume me. I knew I didn't want the money; you can't put a price tag on the hurt that I will have to work through. You can't put "pain and suffering" into a number. I can't prove to anyone what I have mentally and spiritually gone through. I knew, more than anything, that I didn't want justice. I wanted to hurt him so badly that he would remember the day he shook my foundation. I wanted, in that courtroom, for him to remember my name and never forget who he was messing with. I wanted to turn his life towards the worst and upside down.

Chapter 8 – Descend

Overall, none of that is healthy. Even more importantly, none of those feelings were Godly. I was letting my hurt define who I was and my actions. I was allowing my hurt to charge its own path. That is exactly the opposite of what we are supposed to do as Christians. We are supposed to give those who wronged us over to the Lord. He is the eternal Father that we come to, crying and broken into pieces, and He is telling us He will handle it, just let Him.

Immediately, I dropped to my knees, and I started to pray. Not half-heartedly or for my will, but to hear God. To wait on God. I had been going 100 mph. I had told myself that I had forgiven this man. I did, but I knew I had taken it back upon myself to seek revenge. I had allowed him to shake my foundation. This man did shake my foundation. I was and am changed by what happened that day on the plane, but I am still who God says I am. I am still a daughter of the King. I am still worthy. I am still loved. I can still have joy. I can still smile. I can still live.

The access to a computer telling me how I should and could feel made me question God and His plan. So I started to unplug. I started to dive back into God's word because I was more than dehydrated from the time I spent running away from His healing in my life. I had tried to mend my wound on my own, but that didn't work out for me. I tried to work it all out on my own, and I felt ashamed to know that it was resolved until I chose to listen to the world. I had overcome and continued on in my life following passionately after God, and then I slid right back down. I slid into the thoughts of this world and the encouragement of this world.

Chapter 8 – Descend

Listen to me closely. The only words we should hold as Truth is God's Word. I fell into the worldly support I was being given. I had overcome until, at a moment's notice, I had fallen back again into the same hurt and shame. In Romans 12:2 there is this encouragement: "Do not be conformed to this world, but be transformed by the renewal of your mind, that by testing you may discern what is the will of God, what is good and acceptable and perfect." I had fallen into being conformed to this world. On my knees that night, I completely surrendered my hurt to God, never to be picked up once again. Fully given to Him. God was transforming my heart.

I started to pray out loud for the man on the plane once again. I prayed for me to completely give the hurt he caused to God. Then, I started to hear prayers come from my lips that I didn't even recognize as myself. I started to pray for this man who hurt me. I started to pray for his heart to be changed. I started to pray that a Christian would walk into his life and plant a seed. I prayed that he would never lay a hand on another woman the way he did me. I prayed that God would utilize someone one day to allow him to find a personal relationship with Jesus Christ. Finally, I prayed that I would meet him. I prayed to meet him face to face and to tell him what he did. To remind him of what happened. Then, to tell him that I forgave him. I forgive him for what he has done. This was the moment of complete forgiveness for the second time in my journey. The willingness to not hurt him for hurting me. I realized at this moment that I might never meet him, but I pray that he knows that I forgive him.

I started to laugh at myself a little bit, recognizing what felt a little too familiar. I guess it was because I am

Chapter 8 – Descend

stubborn and I have to fall before the Lord multiple times before I give everything. I started to challenge myself to stop holding on to the past, to stop holding on to my hurts, to stop counting the wrongs and start focusing on the goodness of God. Focus on the plans that He has for me. Start to focus on my healing and running back to God. Focus on growing our relationship back to being as strong as possible because even though my foundation was shaken, I am still here. God is my foundation, and He will never let me down.

Standing before my friends at the bottom of the mountain, I knew that every part of the journey was worth it. Every part, excluding nothing. At this point in my relationship with God, I know that it will one day be worth it. All the internal spiritual battles that I went through will be worth it. Even though it took me more than once, I still surrendered it all to God.

I say this to show you that you will not be perfect. No one is unflawed but Jesus. When you start your journey as a Christian, you have a huge motivation to clean house and never to mess up ever again. This feeling and conviction is great, but the reality is we will fall. What matters is how many times we will get back up. How many times we will return to the Lord. How many times we will still cry out to God, broken into pieces, even in our anger and our hurt.

Even as a mature Christian, you may struggle completely surrendering it all to God like me. Keep turning it all back to God. He will never get tired of taking it, but one day you will get tired of picking it back up. Leave it to Jesus. Reflect on your journey and find hope in the fact that you will one day be able to smile. Even if you can't right now, one day you will be able to sit across from someone and

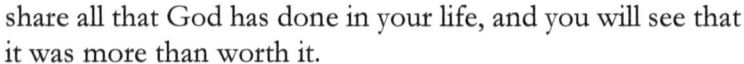

share all that God has done in your life, and you will see that it was more than worth it.

Your current state that you are in should not distract you from what God has called you to do and to be.

Chapter 8 – Descend

CHAPTER 9

Different View

As we were all walking back to the car, the sun started setting. I took a moment to just take a deep breath in and soak up everything one last time. When I was letting it out, I just whispered, "Thank you." I knew I was thanking God. Thanking God for all He was teaching me in this short time. Thanking God for all He had created. Thanking God that He would allow me to see His beauty in creation.

We got in the car to head back to camp, and we saw the other side of the mountain, the opposite side of the one that we had climbed. The other side of the mountain was weathered at an angle that would have been much easier to climb. I pointed this out to my leader and all he responded with was, "I know." I know? He knew all along that there was an easier way, but we didn't take it? This didn't make sense. I had a little internal temper tantrum because I thought it was a waste of time and energy to have gone the long way. Then I couldn't help but burst out laughing because the leader knew. He knew when we wanted to quit that there was an easier way. He knew as I slid, twice, that there was an easier way. But that wasn't the way that he chose for us to go. In the car, I just couldn't help but smile. I knew I had learned to fully trust in God's plan, even if another way seemed to be easier, it wasn't my path to take.

Chapter 9 – Different View

God, the God you and I serve, if you are Christian, loved you so much that He uniquely crafted your story before you were even born. God knows what will happen in your life and He is the only one who knows. We can all plan, starting in middle school when the counselors ask us where we want to go to college and who we want to be. I think it is great to be prepared and work towards who you want to be, but let me tell you that who I wanted to be as a sixth grader is completely different now at twenty years old. The colleges I wanted to apply to in middle school didn't even make the list to apply to in my senior year. The thoughts and dreams of my middle school self could not have imagined what I am living out right now. Please don't get me wrong, it is by nothing I have done, it is all by God's grace. I sit in awe and wonder of how God wanted me to be used. How God has directed my every step. How I have run away from Him and run back crying and broken multiple times. And how God still loves me the same. His unconditional love is overwhelming.

Ask yourself the question, "Who told you?" I love this question so much because it made me pause. Who or what in your life is standing in your way? Who told you that you weren't good enough? Who told you that you aren't old enough? Who told you that you aren't pretty enough? Who told you that you are not worthy? Who told you that you could never work there? Who told you to get your head out of the clouds? Who told you that you are just a bad apple? Who told you that you could never make your dreams a reality? Who told you that you could never amount to be who you want to be? Who caused you to stop believing in yourself? Who told you…?

Chapter 9 – Different View

As I kept running over this question in my mind, it was captivating me. I couldn't stop running it through every part of my brain, and soon it seeped into my heart. Who told you, Jillian? I sat down and reflected on my life, and I remember exactly who told me. I remember exactly who told me every statistic of who I could become. I remember every statistic. Suicide. Pregnant teen. Prostitute. Alone. Drop out. Runaway. All the things that a bunch of fancy calculations said I would fall into a category. I would fall into who the world said I would be. But God. God stepped into the picture. All the things that were just listed don't define a person. If you are in any of those categories, God loves you unconditionally and will never let go of you. He has a purpose for you. I'm so sorry if you didn't see that. I know that I didn't see it.

The day I turned twenty years old fell on a Sunday. I remember waking up in my pink and purse themed room at home. It was fit for my third-grade self, and I just loved waking up to a room that was frozen in time. I soaked it all in like a sponge, like I had never seen any of it before. All of the stuffed animals, awards, pictures, and memories. In my room on that absolutely beautiful sunny day, a day where we are celebrating my birth, I just broke down and cried. The morning of what is supposed to be a very joyful day, I cried. The tears, though they weren't falling due to anger or sadness, fell from my eyes in reverence of who God is and how He has delivered me. He took a broken little girl who knew all too well about shame. Who knew all too well about guilt. God took a broken girl like me, who was supposed to be dead before this very moment. A girl who wasn't supposed to make it to her twenties, and if I did, I was supposed to be on the street selling myself because of the shame that overwhelmed me. I was supposed to be self-

Chapter 9 – Different View

destructing because of the lies of the enemy. I was supposed to be hanging onto that stranger who hurt me on that international flight and give it all up because the world is too much to handle alone. But God. God is the one who brought me to this twentieth birthday. God is the one who washed me clean. God is the one who walked me through every single moment. God is the one I clung to when I thought I was going to throw it all away. God is the one who saved me.

Tears started to rush down my face, and y'all, I am not cute at all when I cry. I just cried and cried. All that escaped my lips was 'thank you.' Thank you, Jesus, for delivering me to this very moment. Thank you, Jesus, for bringing me out of hiding from You when You were with me all along. Thank you, Jesus. I just thought of all things that I could've been. Not to boast, not to be arrogant, not because I think I am better. I thought of who I could've been because that is my life without Jesus Christ in it. Without Jesus in my heart, I would have been lost in plain sight. I would have been trapped in my sin, but all by the power of Jesus Christ, that isn't my story.

I was a self-destructive, shameful, guilty, worthless time bomb ready to explode without Jesus. Romans 5:8 says "but God shows his love for us in that while we were still sinners, Christ died for us." With Him, I am made whole. My guilt and shame have been taken from me, I have worth as the daughter of the Most-High King, and I have eternal life in Jesus Christ. God can transform your story if you let Him. He can use it for His glory if you let Him.

Jesus is the only one who can write my story. He is the only one who knows which chapter holds what. He is the only one who knows my every movement before I have even

Chapter 9 – Different View

made it. God is the one. God is real. God is the only one who can define me. Nothing else. Not my hurt. Not my shame. Not my guilt. Not my pain. Not anger. Not my accomplishments. Not my awards. Nothing can define me but God.

God is the only one who can turn pain into praise. On the morning of my twentieth birthday, all I could do was cry in praise. Jesus, Jesus, Jesus, thank you. Thank you for choosing me. He wanted me, and wants you, too. God defines me. God will lead me. God will orchestrate my steps. (Proverbs 16:9) I will give Him everything not to earn anything, but because I owe Him everything. Even crazier, I owe Him everything, yet He is not a debt collector. God will not force you to praise Him. God will not force you to love Him. God will not force you to come to Him. I want to. I choose to. I praise Him after I have seen what He has done in my life. He has drastically changed a time bomb like me into a shining reflection of who He is. I want to worship. I want to praise Him. I want to shout God's name from the rooftops. I want to be better. I want to love Him more. I want to know Him more. I want to do everything for Him. I will give Him my everything. I will give Him me. I want to be the best shining reflection of His light that I can be by His power. I just want to hear, "Well done, my good and faithful servant." I want to be able to see lives that are broken turn towards Him. I want to start a movement. A movement of people who are authentic. Not wanting to always show the best, most perfect version of themselves. I want a group of people that will sit down and share their struggles, share how they are or were broken, too. But God. A group of people who throw away this false image that you have to be okay. A group of people who aren't always their sparkly best at church. A group of people that can break down in front of

Chapter 9 – Different View

the world to say, "I am nothing without God. I can do nothing without God. I don't even want to try because I have seen where that led me in my past, and God has so much more in store." A group of people that look and say, "It is okay not to be okay. It is okay to question. It is okay to be angry. It is okay to not have everything in your life together. It is more than okay. Come to God as you are, He wants you as you are. But once you believe in Him, don't stay as you are. That is a waste. That is a waste of the new life you have been given. It is a waste of a beautiful purpose that awaits you. Don't wallow or hold on to your past. Claim God's love."

CHAPTER 10

Evidence

As we got back to the camp, we all got out of the car, and it was like we were back to where we started. Almost like everything we had just gone through was a distant memory. Then, as we started to walk, I could feel the adrenaline in me wearing off and the soreness starting to set in.

I started to walk a little funny with a little wobble as I went off to the cabin. I was stopped by a couple of people, and they asked, "Are you okay?" I responded, "Yes, just a little sore." The soreness had caused me to walk a little different, but I was given the opportunity to share with people why I was sore. I could show them my rock from the peak. They could see my semi-fresh cuts on my legs and arms. The beauty in sharing with someone about your hurt after the fact is you are already healing. You are no longer in the trenches of it, you are on the other side. It is no longer the burden you are bearing, but a story to tell.

I was given the awesome advice to "walk with a limp." Immediately I think of when I was on crutches, wobbling around to move from place to place. In fact, I know walking with limp all too well.

When I was a seventh-grade cheerleader, basketball player, and track runner, I broke my right ankle. Still to this

Chapter 10 – Evidence

day, I don't know what exact moment caused the break, but when all of my adrenaline left towards the end of the day, the pain was enormous. I remember the phone call that I had to make to my mom. "Mom… I think I hurt my ankle." My mom is my person. Someone who will be there as soon as possible, rain or shine, no matter what they are doing. Well, sure enough, she picked me up from the school as soon as possible and brought me to the Emergency Room. Several scans later and several doctors later I found out that I had a hairline fracture in my right ankle.

The next day I had to go to the orthopedist. This is the doctor that lays out all of the cool colors and patterns you can possibly have for your cast. I remember wanting a cool color that everyone would want to sign. I got purple to match my school colors, purple and gold. Then, they gave me crutches, those dreaded crutches, and I went on my way.

Before this moment, I had never broken or hurt a bone in my life. Although I had played with my friend's crutches and sibling's crutches, I figured out that it is entirely different when you have your own crutches. You can't have fun and swing back and forth on them. You can't get tired of playing with them and give them back. When they are your crutches, you have to use them until the doctor releases you into a walking boot.

The pain that comes with using crutches every day is directly below your armpit. It is a stinging pain. I never realized how much this hurt until I experienced it for myself. My mom pointed out that I could put stuffed animals or towels on the top of the crutches and try to make them more bearable. My mom was always seeing the light in situations and trying to make every situation fun for me, so I believed

Chapter 10 – Evidence

her. We got old rags and duct tape and started to work on my crutches. By the end of our crutch craft project, I think I had a pair of the best looking crutches I had ever seen.

The next day when I had to go to school, I started using my improved crutches, but I realized the stinging pain was still there. Part of it was a memory of the pain, but the improved crutch still irritated my side.

I know you all are probably thinking, 'why is she telling me about her crutches from middle school?' The reason is all of us have a crutch. The overall crutch in our lives is sin. The way sin presents itself can be completely different for each one of us. We all have sinned. The Bible says "For all have sinned and fallen short of the glory of God" in Romans 3:23. This verse is so true.

If our universal crutch is a sin, and everyone has it, then everyone should know how it feels. Sadly though, some people want to cover up that they ever had crutches. They want to pretend that they never used crutches and got better by their own will and strength. This is ridiculous.

My point is that we all have sinned. No one is perfect. The only perfect person was fully man and fully God and His name is Jesus. All the rest of us are either sinners who reject God or sinners who have gone to God and said, "Look, I know I have messed up. Actually, I know I have messed up so much that I could never be good enough to get into Heaven on my own. Thank you, Jesus, that You are my Savior. That You are the bridge to allow me to get into Heaven. Jesus, I know you died for my sins and the world's sins on the cross. I know that You died, but You didn't stay dead. You rose again on the third day! Jesus, You have

Chapter 10 – Evidence

defeated death! Now, with You on my side, I pray that You help me hate sin. Not some sin, but all sin." When you pray the prayer of accepting the precious gift of Jesus into your life, then you are saved. (Romans 10:9)

As believers, we look back on who we once were. We are not "above" sin now that we are saved. We are saved by grace through faith. We were given the gift of eternal life that we chose to accept.

Again, our universal crutch is sin, although Satan chooses different ways for us to fall. Satan studies us to find out our weakest point and then uses that. When we do fall, it results in us being different than who we once were. This is our limp.

I want to encourage us all to walk with a limp. My fall was the shame and guilt I had to carry. If I walk with a limp, inevitably someone will come up to me and ask what happened? I will be able to tell them the story of who I once was. I am not the same person anymore because God has restored me and made me new.

Walking with a limp exemplifies how we, as Christians, can be authentic with others about how we are doing in our own lives. We have two reasons to walk with a limp. The first is to show others that you have been there, too. Other people will be able to see that you are not perfect, and you immediately become more approachable. They see that your life isn't always picture perfect and they are encouraged that they will be able to make it one day, too. The second option is to walk with a limp because you are struggling and need help. As a body of believers, none of us should suffer in silence. We should have a support system

Chapter 10 – Evidence

within the church and people that are walking through life with us. When they catch that we are limping, they should immediately turn us to God's Word as well as pray over us and our situation.

The person that exemplifies walking with a limp in my eyes is Paul. In fact, one of my favorite people in the Bible is Paul. In 2 Corinthians 11:22-30 Paul writes, "Are they Hebrews? So am I. Are they Israelites? So am I. Are they offspring of Abraham? So am I. Are they servants of Christ? I am a better one—I am talking like a madman—with far greater labors, far more imprisonments, with countless beatings, and often near death. Five times I received at the hands of the Jews the forty lashes less one. Three times I was beaten with rods. Once I was stoned. Three times I was shipwrecked; a night and a day I was adrift at sea; on frequent journeys, in danger from rivers, danger from robbers, danger from my own people, danger from Gentiles, danger in the city, danger in the wilderness, danger at sea, danger from false brothers; in toil and hardship, through many a sleepless night, in hunger and thirst, often without food, in cold and exposure. And, apart from other things, there is the daily pressure on me of my anxiety for all the churches. Who is weak, and I am not weak? Who is made to fall, and I am not indignant? If I must boast, I will boast of the things that show my weakness." Paul, in this passage of Scripture, is standing in the midst of all of these false teachers and Pharisees. They are all bragging about how they are better than the person next to them. The conversation is turned to Paul, and he basically tells them everything he has done wrong in his life and all the ways he has been persecuted. He tells them how he has fallen and how he didn't do anything right. Paul was at a point in his life where, even if he wanted to do right, he couldn't. Then, he stops his rant of everything

Chapter 10 – Evidence

wrong he has done and how he will boast in his "weakness." This simple word changed my life, and I believe it should change Christians, churches, and you personally like it did me. It transformed me 180 degrees. Paul stops all of the bragging and the pride that is happening to say I am the worst, but God.

I love Paul so much because I know I am Paul. I fall into sin all the time. I know as a Christian we identify with the moment where we accepted Christ into our lives. That should be the ultimate turning point in our lives, but sometimes it's not. I would dare to say most of the time it's not. I feel like we are hiding behind a veil of shame and brokenness. As Christians we are afraid to exclaim, "I am messed up!" We act as though in that moment after accepting Jesus into our hearts, we have to be instantly and drastically changed inside and out without any work. I know now that this is far from the truth.

What Jesus did on the cross is an amazing work. God allowed the impossible to become possible. Jesus died and rose again on the third day. This is a miracle that should never be downplayed, ever. When we get to a point in our lives where we accept this gift that God has given us, we are saved. We are now going to Heaven, and we have the Holy Spirit inside of us. Although the brutal reality is the baggage that you had ten minutes ago, you still have. The sin you were drowning in, is still there. The shame and guilt you feel will come back. This sounds like I am trying to rob the joy from you, but that is far from the truth. The truth is the pain, guilt, shame, sin, hurt, and all of it will still be there after you become a Christian. What is radically different is that it is no longer your burden to carry. So many times in our lives we face situations where we look and we think, "I can't do it all."

Chapter 10 – Evidence

Well, as a believer, we are not meant to. One more time: we are not meant to carry the burden. We are designed to leave it at the feet of Jesus. This task sounds very simple. I just need to leave my schooling, grades, future, relationships, family life, and all of my baggage at the feet of Jesus and it will all be okay. Yes, yes it will.

There is a second step: leave it there. Leave all of your burdens and baggage at the feet of the cross. That is what allows you to walk away different. That is what transforms your life, and you are no longer conforming to the world. You take a drastic step of realizing your situation didn't change just because you became a follower of Christ, but your game plan should have done a 180. You can leave all your worries, shame, and hurt with God and He will handle it.

I know the constant battle with worry well. I remember many sleepless nights in college going to bed worrying. I was anxious about the different financial aid award letters and acceptances. I was basking in the uncertainty of which college I would go to and the ability to even afford the one I chose. I was looking up at the mountain in front of me that was not moving or shrinking, the mountain of a decision of deciding what is next in my life. Where will I go next? Well, the reason I worried and felt so overwhelmed was because the weight of the world was on my shoulders. I was not giving my situation to God.

We all do this so many times. Whether it is our relationship or our marriage, our job or our school, our family or our friends, we hold the weight, and we feel like we are about to break underneath all of the pressure, but we still don't change anything we are doing. Well, God is looking on

Chapter 10 – Evidence

with arms opened wide, waiting for you to give it all to Him. Just give it all to Him.

When I figured out that was the magic secret, I couldn't explain my experience. The word that comes to my mind is 'peace.' A silent, frozen, breathtaking peace surrounded me. It was like I knew that everything was taken care of. I could have hit my teenage self in the face, and said "Why did you spend all of that time struggling and worrying? You could have just given it all to God!" Well, to be honest, I still struggle with this. I would like to think I give it all to God, but when I do, I want to take it back. I want to act like I am fully trusting in God, but I just want to take a few things off of God's plate.

In school, you are provided with planners. The teachers then teach you how to write down everything. Then, when you complete the task, you can cross it off. Sometimes there is a lot to do, and other times it is like there is nothing going on around you. I am the type of person that when I have nothing on my plate, I start borrowing other people's tasks. The empty planner doesn't seem correct to me. I feel like I need to look around and see what other people might be doing that I could be doing because obviously, I am doing something wrong when I don't have anything scheduled to do.

I am the exact same way spiritually. And I HATE it. I will give God everything and feel His overwhelming peace. I find immediate joy and relief that He has helped me. Then, later down the road, it is like I forgot the unmeasurable burden that God has just saved me from and I start to act like I can help God. Yes, it is completely silly. Me? Help God? But that is the exact way I act. I go back to Him and I

Chapter 10 – Evidence

start to think, "I don't need to give you my grades because I still need to work hard. I still need to be able to maintain a high grade point average to be accepted into colleges and earn scholarships. Also, I don't need to give you my appearance. I know I have been struggling with weight and I need to eat healthy. I can handle self-criticism. Self-criticism is what motivates me to be better. Then I will eat healthier, workout, and end up losing weight. So God, You don't need to worry about that one anymore, I got it." I keep doing this and doing this until I have taken back everything or most everything I gave to God in the first place. This seems counteractive, only because it is.

I want to challenge you, but not only you, me too, to stop holding onto a burden that is no longer ours to bear. God is waiting to take it from you. He wants to hold it and deal with it for you. We need to let Him. More importantly, we need to let Him do His job. We can't keep going back and taking what we just gave God.

God created us, not the other way around. We are made to be a vessel to be used by God for His glory. God does not work for us, He is not just some side help that we hired to take a little load off. He is almighty, all-powerful, and worthy to be praised. We need to stop and be grateful, truly grateful, that He will bear our burdens for us because He doesn't have to. He chooses to because of His unconditional love for us.

Next time you are faced with a trial or temptation – the mountains in our lives – I pray that you will be able to seek God first and foremost. I pray you see that the road to overcoming things of this world is not easy. We may fall, and we may slip, but we have other Christians to encourage us and help us along the way. God is with us the whole time to guide our every step, we just have to be in tune with His presence. I hope with everything in me that you see your strength does not come from your own might. Your battle is not with things that are seen but with what is unseen. (2 Corinthians 10:4) You are in a spiritual battle. Equip yourself with the full armor of God, prayer, accountability partners, and fix your eyes on the one true God. (Ephesians 6:11-12; Hebrews 12:2) Choose to walk authentically in your faith to encourage others who may not understand how you can continue on, so they may continue on with you. Then, one day, the next mountain you face will not be something to be endured, it will be a testimony in the making. You will be able to bask in the promise that when we are weak, Christ is strong. (2 Corinthians 12:9-10) You are no longer striving in this world by the grit of your teeth, but weightlessly praising God with each of your steps. Finally, completely understanding that the burden is not ours to bear, but God is willing to take it upon Himself, we can be vulnerable and authentic with those around us when we hit a valley in life, allowing them the opportunity to point us back to God. In the midst of the best and worst times, hold on to our hope and joy because we know that God is working for our good, we just don't see the end result yet.

Powerfully Weak

Me at the top of the mountain.

ABOUT JILLIAN MURPHY

I love dancing, shopping, and talking about Jesus. Spending quality time with people I love is time well spent (and if there is food involved that's definitely a plus)! Taking a moment to soak in everything around me and belly laughing through life is what I do. I was born in Oklahoma, but raised in Texas! I am one of four kids, and my mama is my inspiration, role model, and best friend. Oh, and I have a sweet puppy named Jonah!

I always introduce myself as "Just Jillian." I know it's because I see how big and awesome of a God I serve. I am super blessed that He chose me to use as a vessel. I strive to use each moment of my life to reflect His love for people. I love speaking and writing about what God has taught me in my life so far. My goal is to inspire other women to live an authentic life as a Christian so that their faith in Christ inspires non-believers to trust in God. We have all messed up, but we have a God that wants to scoop us up right where we are!

I realized my call to ministry during the Summer of 2014 on a mission trip to Washington, D.C. The following fall, I followed God's plan for my life by interning at a women's safe house in Dallas, TX, Restored Hope Ministries. Currently, my long-term goal is to establish a women's safe house on the foundation of Jesus Christ and have a free health clinic as an extension of that safe house.

God allowed me to publish my first book *"The Four Seasons of Hope"* in July 2016, while I was still in high school. In 2017, Mike Rodriguez asked me to join him as a co-author for *"A Bigger Purpose,"* and I had the opportunity to write a chapter about "The Power of Prayer." Most recently, I released my new best-selling faith-based book, *"This is WHY"* in June 2017. Through ministry, I continue to use my gift of writing to encourage believers and convince non-believers to trust Him.

I have fallen head over heels in love with ministering to women. My favorite part is being able to pour all that I have learned into those around me. I fully believe that we are all like cups: we should be filled with the Word of God and pour out as we disciple others. My goal is to always have someone pouring into me, and simultaneously I pour into others, so that name of Jesus is proclaimed.

My ultimate goal is to keep pointing others towards Christ, and I continually pray, "Less of me and more You, Lord." I strive to keep spreading the good news of Jesus Christ while trying to live a life as a reflection of Him. Stay tuned for my journey!

Jillian Murphy

Powerfully Weak

Powerfully Weak

Powerfully Weak

Powerfully Weak

Disclaimer & Copyright Information

Some of the events, locales, and conversations have been recreated from memories. In order to maintain their anonymity, in some instances, the names of individuals and places have been changed. As such, some identifying characteristics and details may have changed.

Although the author and publishers have made every effort to ensure that the information in this book was correct at press time, the authors and publishers do not assume and hereby disclaim any liability to any party for any loss, damage, or disruption caused by errors or omissions, whether such errors or omissions result from negligence, accident, or any other cause. The author is solely responsible for the content of this story.

All quotes, unless otherwise noted,
are attributed to the Author or to the Holy Bible.

Cover illustration, book design, and production
Copyright © 2018 by Tribute Publishing LLC
www.TributePublishing.com

Scripture references are copyrighted by www.BibleGateway.com
which is operated by the Zondervan Corporation, L.L.C

NOTES

NOTES

www.ingramcontent.com/pod-product-compliance
Lightning Source LLC
Chambersburg PA
CBHW020427010526
44118CB00010B/452